James Field Spalding

The Teaching and Influence of Saint Augustine

An Essay with Particular Reference to Recent Misapprehensions

James Field Spalding

The Teaching and Influence of Saint Augustine
An Essay with Particular Reference to Recent Misapprehensions

ISBN/EAN: 9783337336431

Printed in Europe, USA, Canada, Australia, Japan

Cover: Foto ©Lupo / pixelio.de

More available books at **www.hansebooks.com**

THE
TEACHING AND INFLUENCE

OF

SAINT AUGUSTINE

AN ESSAY

WITH PARTICULAR REFERENCE TO RECENT MISAPPREHENSIONS

BY

JAMES FIELD SPALDING

RECTOR OF CHRIST CHURCH, CAMBRIDGE, MASS.

NEW YORK
JAMES POTT AND COMPANY
1886

COPYRIGHT, 1886,
BY JAMES FIELD SPALDING.

ELECTROTYPED AND PRINTED
BY RAND, AVERY, AND COMPANY,
BOSTON, MASS.

Below are given the principal works and editions referred to in the following pages: —

Sancti Aurelii Augustini Hipponensis Episcopi Opera omnia. Opera et studiis monachorum ordinis Sancti Benedicti. (Parisiis, 1836.)

Library of the Fathers. New issue. (Oxford and London, 1879.)

The Works of Aurelius Augustine, Bishop of Hippo. A new translation. (Edinburgh, 1876.)

Select Anti-Pelagian Treatises of St. Augustine, with an Introduction by William Bright, D.D. (Oxford, 1880.)

A Treatise on the Augustinian Doctrine of Predestination. By J. B. Mozley, D.D. Third edition. (London, 1883.)

Histoire de Saint Augustin. Par M. Poujoulat. (Paris, 1846.)

Der heilige Augustinus, dargestellt von Carl Bindemann. (Greifswald, 1869.)

Evenings with the Skeptics. By John Owen, Rector of East Anstey, Devon. (London, 1881.)

The Continuity of Christian Thought. By Alexander V. G. Allen, Professor in the Episcopal Theological School in Cambridge, Mass. (Boston, 1884.)

THE TEACHING AND INFLUENCE OF SAINT AUGUSTINE

ONE result of the Catholic revival which has visited the Church of England, and indeed the entire Anglican Communion, during the present century, has been to awaken and renew interest in the study of the Fathers. The appeal so continually made to antiquity has been taken up and carried on from one point to another in our modern life; and it can be no matter of surprise, but should be cause for deep gratitude, that it has met so full and hearty a response. Sincerity of spirit, earnestness of purpose, and patience in actual research have led honest inquirers to satisfactory results. The wisdom, learning, intellectual grasp, spiritual perception, or clear insight into Holy Scripture; the profound reasoning, soaring imagination, or acute speculation of these ancient writers has been marked and admired. Although, from the very necessities of the case, they have been judged far inferior in some ways to modern writers, in others they have been found to be as far superior to them. In thought and expression and philosophical theory it has been seen again and again that they have anticipated the moderns, and readers have been surprised to find that what they supposed was original to the nineteenth century was in the writings of the first or second. More than all else, the practical *consensus* of antiquity upon cardinal matters of doctrine, or discipline, or worship, has yielded testimony which has been invaluable; and the Church's teachings, seen in this concentrated light of ancient interpretation, have come to be more definitely discerned, and her holy ways more devoutly loved. If a wholly different animus has appeared to actuate any in their investigations, as may be noticed in certain recent writings about the Fathers, even this has not been without advantage. The extreme of inaccuracy of statement or fancifulness of conjecture, the farthest reach of free-thinking in aversion to Catholic dogma or sacramental grace or the authority of the Church, — all this has been but a strong incentive to urge many who never before inquired to look into the Fathers for themselves, and see whether these things were so. Not seldom the arguments of detractors have overshot themselves and proved too much, and thinking men have been content to say that it was very strange that this or that great Doctor of the Church should have been held in universal esteem for so many centuries, for the grandness and comprehensiveness of his teaching, and that his real place of littleness and bigotry should be the discovery of to-day!

Moreover, the differences and the agreements between the earlier and the later Fathers, or between the

Greek and the Latin Fathers, have been put under examination. While there have been found natural variations, such as one would expect, from the distinction between the Eastern and the Western type of mind, habits of thought, surroundings, or climatic influence; or as between the first century and the fourth or fifth, in the advancement of civilization, the growth of the Church, or the power of the State, a thorough investigation, as we believe, has not revealed those radical differences which some have claimed between the orthodox East and the orthodox West; — as if the Greek and the Latin theologies had *nothing in common* upon the broad, underlying truths, e.g. of the presence of God in the world or in the Church, the Incarnation of our Lord, Divine grace, human sin and human freedom.

Confessedly pre-eminent among the Latin Fathers, — many would say among all the Fathers, — is S. Augustine. His natural gifts and acquired powers were so remarkable, the extent and variety of his writings so great; his impress upon his own age was so weighty, his authority throughout the Western Church for the next thousand years so unshaken; and the range of his subsequent influence has been so wide and deep, that history has brought down to our day no name among Illustrious Christian thinkers and teachers so familiar.

In this very fact, with what it implies, lies the secret of our desire to say something anew upon his life and work. The familiarity with the name of S. Augustine is, of course, on the part of very many, even intelligent people, in this busy age, only that, — *a familiarity with the name;* they live, all unconsciously, under the power of his master-spirit. Others, again, both in the Church and in the dissenting bodies about us, have a more or less mistaken conception of this great saint and Father: — they almost take away his individuality, and identify him in their minds with Luther, or Calvin, or Jansen ; while they think of his teaching as chiefly some dreadful notions of predestination and original sin and eternal punishment. Both these classes of people need to gain a knowledge of S. Augustine. Others still, who years ago may have been careful students of his writings, may find benefit in observing, from the new perspective, of present individual experience or of the ideas of our time, the relative proportions of his opinions and doctrines; having learned, perhaps, with fuller knowledge and riper wisdom, to put a fairer estimate upon his life and work ; to enter, with more sensitive appreciation, into his spirit ; more accurately to understand his teaching; and thus, more truly than ever before, to comprehend his greatness.

One other object we have in view;— to say a few words upon *the influence* of S. Augustine. We do not regard that influence in the distant past and up to the present hour either as unmixed evil, or as more evil than good. Accordingly, we should not think with satisfaction of what has been called "the lingering hold of Augustine upon the modern mind." Nor do we see any reason to suppose that his influence is really waning. We believe that the centuries to come will fully uphold the just verdict of the present and the past,—— not of blind admiration, or servile following, or unquestioning assent; but of glad recognition of unwonted powers of mind and heart loyally and on the whole wisely exercised, in defence of great doctrines of Holy Scripture, and in maintenance of the ministry and sacraments of the Church. That he committed no error of doctrine, we do not say; he never claimed infallibility for himself; in his humility he was farthest from any such pretence; he is not our master, nor has the Church ever accepted all his system of doctrine; as has been justly observed, " she is free from all bondage to the letter of his writings; she is not his, but he is hers."

We do not propose to speak with any fulness of S. Augustine's life; yet, even at the risk of repeating what may be known, we shall trace its main events; for the history of his life is wonderfully bound up with the history of his opinions. He was born at Thagaste, in Numidia, November 13, A.D. 354. His father, Patricius, was then a heathen.[1] His mother, Monica, was a devout Christian. His father's opposition may have prevented his being baptized in infancy. His mother did all she could; and made him a catechumen by the ceremonies then in use in the Church.[2] When he was quite

---

[1] He became a Christian late in life, won by the example and persuasion of the holy Monica.

[2] In Wall's *Hist. of Inf. Baptism*, Vol. I. p. 403, etc., a fair explanation is given why Augustine was not baptized in infancy, in answer to the supposition that infant baptism was not then practised.

a young child, he was near being baptized, at his own request, in serious illness; but on his recovery the sacrament was again postponed, in part, now, from his mother's wish, who foresaw the temptations of youth, and dreaded the greater guilt of sin after baptism. (*Confess.* l. i. c. 11.) In spite of her fond instructions, his boyhood soon showed an extraordinary degree of waywardness. He hated his studies, and had to be whipped to his tasks. Latin he naturally acquired with ease, and more from listening than from lessons (*Conf.* i. 14); and he has left on record his exceeding love for that language; but all else was "a burden and a punishment," and emphatically the Greek tongue, for which he seems to have continued to cherish a dislike, and in which he never gained high proficiency; although his ignorance was not such as to justify the contemptuous statements which have been made upon the subject.[1] At the age of sixteen we find him, after having been for a time at school in Madaura, a neighboring city, spending a year at home, while his parents saved money to send him to Carthage to complete his studies. That year of "imposed idleness" must have been one of great peril to him, just at that age, and with such a nature and habits as he had. His *Confessions* tell of the development of vice which then went on within

[1] His own admissions of slight knowledge, — "prope nihil" he calls it in one place, should be taken in connection with passages in his writings which prove the extent of that knowledge. A great number of such have been collected by Abp. Trench in his *S. Augustine as an Interpreter of Scripture*, pp. 20-22. For his own statements, cf. *Conf.* i. 13,.14; *Con. lit. Petil.* ii. 38; *De Trin.* iii. 1; *De Doctr. Christ.* ii. 11-15.

him. His father seems not to have been much concerned, and his mother's warnings and entreaties were only despised (*Conf.* ii. 3), though both were but "too anxious" that he should get learning, the one with motive of worldly advancement, the other to bring him nearer God. Soon after this his father died; and the subsequent expense of his education was partly met by a wealthy fellow-townsman. His student-life of three years in Carthage (from seventeen to nineteen) was one of gay, wild, licentious dissipation, and yet of high attainment in his studies. He shone especially in rhetoric, (a department which included far more then than now,) and found himself at the head of the school. (*Conf.* iii. 3.) The reading of Cicero's *Hortensius* first awakened in him the love of philosophy. Urged by the spirit of that book, and doubtless recalling his early Christian instructions, he began to look into the Holy Scriptures; but soon turned away, not thinking them worthy to be compared with the dignity of Cicero. (*Conf.* iii. 5.) His attention was next taken by Manichaeism, whose claim of divine inspiration and promises of knowledge and truth (*Conf.* iii. 6; vi. 5) proved a ready snare; and, once captured, he was held for nine years. He embraced this heresy just at the close of his student-life. Returning to his native town, to teach rhetoric, his zeal was at once shown for the success of his new opinions; and he was increasingly elated with pride that by his dialectic skill he could overcome any opponents. Among others, he had won over to Manichaeism a friend whom he had known from a child.

This friend fell sick; he was baptized into the Christian faith; he rebuked the error of Augustine; he died. His death filled Augustine's soul with grief; and the circumstances may have also created a longing for a comfort in grief which perhaps the Christian faith would supply. In his revulsion of feeling he left Thagaste and went back to Carthage. Here he remained several years, "for love of gain making sale of loquacity," as he afterwards describes it.[1] His dissatisfaction with Manichaeism was all this while increasing; he saw, more and more, that its doctrines of God and the world, and especially of evil and its nature, were vain delusions. As a system, it had not kept its promises of wisdom and truth; and when at last he got no answer to his difficulties in a long-desired conference with Faustus, their most distinguished bishop, he became disgusted with the sect, and determined to abandon it. This was in his twenty-ninth year. (*Conf.* v. 3, 7.) Very soon after (probably in A.D. 383), contrary to his mother's wishes, and deceiving her at the time of his going (*Conf.* v. 8), he removed to Rome, in response to inducements of friends, who represented that in that city he would gain higher honors and advantages, and chiefly that he would have a more quiet set of students. There, not unnaturally, from his connection with the sect, he still associated with the Manichaeans. But his defence of their opinions must have been only outward. The fact is he was utterly unsettled, "hopeless of find-

---

[1] At this time, in his twenty-seventh year, he wrote his first work *De apto et pulchro*, which has been lost.

ing the truth" (*Conf.* v. 10), and, knowing not what to think or believe about God or himself, he was already half inclined to fall in with the supposed views of the Academics, and doubt everything. Almost immediately on his arrival he had been visited with a serious illness. After his recovery, he soon found that the students here were quite as undesirable as those at Carthage, though in a different way; and so he was very glad of an opportunity which now offered of taking a public professorship of rhetoric at Milan, and thither he came.

Here he was most kindly received by S. Ambrose, the Bishop of that see, whose influence was to be so powerful in bringing him to the Christian faith. At first Ambrose's eloquence charmed him; then his explanations of Scripture won him; and he gradually found, to his mingled shame and joy, that for so many years he had been opposing an utter misrepresentation of Christianity, — "barking, not against the Catholic faith, but against the parables of carnal imaginations." (*Conf.* vi. 3.) But he was no little time in being brought even thus far. Entirely renouncing Manichaeism (*Conf.* v. 14; vi. 1), much inclined towards the Academics, who "long detained him tossing in the waves" (*De Beata Vita*, 4), and actually becoming again a catechumen, this was only "until something certain should show itself to him." (*Conf.* v. 14.) He continued long in the darkness of universal scepticism, in utter despair of ever finding the truth within or without the Church. (*Conf.* v. 13; vi. 1.) Even when he was made to see his past misapprehensions, through fear he kept holding back from *assenting to anything;* and so his soul, "which could not be healed but by believing, lest it should believe falsehoods refused to be cured." (*Conf.* vi. 4.) It must be owned that he was now largely convinced, intellectually, by *the extent of the authority* of the Holy Scriptures and of the Christian faith throughout the world (*Conf.* vi. 5, 11); and this test of *authority* came to have an increasing weight with him, and to be always put *before reason in the demand for faith.*[1] But the moral nature of Augustine needed a thorough renovation. He admits he was followed more and more closely by a Divine mercy which he knew not;—"I became more wretched, and Thou nearer" (*Conf.* vi. 16); while the fear of death and the judgment which never left him, alone recalled him "from a yet deeper abyss of carnal pleasures." (*Id.*) It is a most sad picture to contemplate; and it must ever be a wonder that his high gifts and powers, now so degraded and defiled, were not utterly destroyed by his licentious indulgence. His hot, passionate temperament even from youth seems never to have been restrained from the fulfilment of sensual desires. For these many years he had been "befouling the spring of friendship with the filth of concupiscence." (*Conf.* iii. 1.) While a student at Carthage, he had become a father; and his son he had piously (?) named Adeodatus. His mother had often desired marriage for him; now her plans seemed likely to succeed; he sent back to Africa the mother of his child; but, having become so base a slave to carnal lust,

---

[1] Cf. *Ep.* cxviii. 32.

he could not wait for the maiden whom he was to marry;
and ended in only putting away one mistress to take
another. (*Conf.* vi. 12, 15.) And all this time, while
his "sins were being multiplied," his intellect was
soaring to loftiest heights of speculation upon religious
questions, of the nature of God and the soul, of incarnation and redemption, of the origin of evil, of the
authority of Scripture, of the bounds of reason and
faith, etc.—all which were to him thus far *only speculative questions*. But God was leading him. The Pla-
tonic (or perhaps more strictly Neo-Platonic) doctrines
proved an efficient awakening influence. In this philosophy, which he ever after considered to be the best
of the old systems and to contain deep spiritual wisdom,
he now found a mighty incentive. It was so rich in
truth, — and yet it stopped just short of what he most
needed, — the great truth of the Incarnation, the humility of the Lord Jesus, the Word made flesh! So Pla-
tonism moved Augustine to turn again to the Holy
Scriptures, and especially to S. Paul's Epistles (*Conf.*
vii. 21); and this time it was to find in God's Word,
under the interpretation of the Church, the divine
foundation of faith, the all powerful motive to a holy
life. We need not dwell upon the further incidents
previous to his conversion. He could no longer say he
had no clear perception of truth; "now it was certain"
(*Conf.* viii. 5), he was convinced, he was persuaded.
The lower animal desires, and these alone, made him
continue to hesitate a little longer; and they had a
wonderful power over him to the very day of his con-

version; but at last, after many violent struggles, coming to a firm purpose on this point, and willing resolutely and thoroughly (*Conf.* viii. 8), through deep anguish and many tears and prayers, the conflict was ended in submission and peace. When we think of what Augustine's career had been thus far, it is not strange that, in the mighty reaction which came upon him, he should have adopted henceforth the celibate and the ascetic life. "Thou didst so convert me unto Thyself," he says, "that I sought neither a wife nor any other of this world's hopes." (*Conf.* viii. 12.) Herein his case is not to be made a law or guide for others; any more than his subsequent peculiar teachings upon marriage need be accepted in their entireness.

Augustine's conversion took place in the summer of A.D. 386. Resigning his professorship as soon as vacation gave him opportunity, he spent some months in retirement with certain of his friends at a villa a few miles out of the city. Here he composed his treatises *Contra Academicos, De Ordine, De Beata Vita,* and the *Soliloquiorum duo Libri.* He was baptized by S. Ambrose, in his church in Milan, on Easter-eve, the 25th of April, A.D. 387, and with him his son Adeodatus and one of his most intimate friends Alypius. His mother was the happy witness of his baptism, rejoicing in the answer to her many prayers. They determined to return to their native country; but at the port of Ostia, Monica, who felt that she had no more to live for, now that her son had become a Catholic Christian, fell ill and died. Changing his plans, Augustine remained in Rome until the next year, and wrote the *De quantitate animae*, the greater part of the *De moribus Ecclesiae Catholicae et de moribus Manichaeorum*, and began the *De Libero Arbitrio*, which he finished some years later, (A.D. 395.) In the summer of A.D. 388 he returned to Thagaste, where he founded a small religious community, at whose head he continued for three years; during this period writing the *De Genesi contra Manichaeos*, *De Musica*, *De Magistro*, and *De Vera Religione*. The fame of his ability and devotion soon spread. He was eagerly sought, for more active labors; and in A.D. 391, against his own wishes, according to a custom then prevalent, he was ordained a priest by Valerius, Bishop of Hippo, for service in the church of that city. Here his eloquence in preaching was equalled only by his loving zeal for the Church, and his power in controversy against her mistaken opponents. Besides discharging the duties of the priesthood, he now found time to write several exegetical works, as well as the important treatises against the Manichaeans, *De Utilitate Credendi*, and *De duabus Animabus*, and the *Disputatio contra Fortunatum*.[1] In A.D. 395, at the age of forty-one, he was consecrated Bishop, as coadjutor to Valerius,[2] who died after a few months, leaving him Bishop of Hippo. From the time

[1] This tract Milman thinks "gives the fairest view of the real controversy" with the Manichaeans. *History of Christianity*, Vol. II. p. 278.

[2] From Ep. ccxiii., written in A.D. 426, we learn that both Valerius and himself were ignorant of the inconsistency of the consecration of coadjutor bishops with the injunction of the 8th Canon of the Council of Nice.

of his ordination to the priesthood, he had continued the mode of living in religious community, which he had established at Thagaste. Now, as Bishop, with his clergy about him, he maintained great plainness of food and dress, and even in his ministrations is said to have refused to wear costly vestments.

We cannot dwell upon the long episcopate of S. Augustine. It became more and more celebrated, until his was the great name throughout the Western Church. This wide reputation came principally from his zeal and ability in defence of Christian doctrine. His philosophical spirit, logical acumen, and dialectical skill, wonderfully helped by a glowing imagination and most facile use of language, with a foundation of considerable learning, and certainly of deep spiritual comprehension of Scripture, proved powerful means of winning multitudes to Christian allegiance, and mighty weapons against the opposition of heresy and schism. He had himself gone through dreadful conflicts with sin and doubt, in coming to the peace and stability of Christianity. He had some definite idea of what the Christian faith and the Christian Church, sin and salvation, Divine grace and human frailty meant. Living in a time of intense worldliness and of real decline of spirituality, of dissension and open strife among those who called themselves Christians, and of the lingering power of paganism upon all classes of society, he deemed the promotion of a right Christian belief and of a Christian living which legitimately flowed therefrom, not a mere matter of opinion, but one of divinely revealed obligation, — one which he ought to urge with all the powers which God had given him. Known eminently from that day to this as a controversialist, his place of honor as a theologian, and the wide and full range of his abilities as a teacher in the Church cannot be questioned.

We naturally find his mature energies first directed against the Manichaeans, from whose snares he had recently escaped. In addition to the treatises which he had already written, he now produced other and more extensive works against them ; among which may be mentioned the *Contra Epistolam Manichaei quam vocant fundamenti*, the long work *Contra Faustum*, in 23 books, the *De Natura Boni*, and the *Contra Secundinum*, which last was his own preference among his writings against Manichaeism. (*Retract.* ii. 10.)

In opposition to the Donatist schism, its unscriptural doctrines and fanatical practices, he wrote a number of works, mostly between the years 400 and 412 ; the principal ones being the *Contra Epistolam Parmeniani*, *De Baptismo*, *Contra literas Petiliani*, and the *De Unitate Ecclesiae*.

Perhaps of more distinct significance than any of the works hitherto named, — certainly of much more wide-reaching influence in the history of Christian doctrine, were his writings against Pelagianism. These were some sixteen in number, called out, one after another, by the exigency of the situation, from A.D. 412 on to the close of his life in A.D. 430, — one being left unfinished. The very titles of most of these works show the general nature of their contents, and the greatness of the subjects considered; e.g. *De Spiritu et litera, De natura et gratia, De perfectione justitiae hominis, De gratia Christi, De peccato originali, De anima et ejus origine, De gratia et libero arbitrio, De correptione et gratia, De praedestinatione sanctorum, De dono perseverantiae.*

Along with these writings against Manichaeans and Donatists, and the early part of those against the Pelagians, S. Augustine was producing also many miscellaneous short treatises, upon various topics of faith and morals, too numerous even for enumeration here, but which are of much value, and have had a lasting reputation: his extensive exegetical works, chiefly upon the Psalms and upon the writings of S. John, formed part of his labor; he was constantly preaching, and some four hundred well authenticated sermons of his have come down to us; moreover, there have been preserved more than two hundred of his Epistles, many of which were elaborate monographs.

We do not forget, and we would make special reference to three other great works of his, either one of which would have enshrined his name in perpetual remembrance. Surely S. Augustine's was not only an industrious life, that, with all the cares of his Episcopate, he could write so fully as we have already stated; but it was the life of a man of remarkable genius, wonderful richness of mind, and depth of spiritual insight, which could produce the *Confessiones*, the *De Trinitate*, and the *De Civitate Dei.* The *Confessiones* were written about the year 400 (some say 397). The *De Trinitate*, which many have thought to be the loftiest work of his genius, occupied him at least sixteen years, from A.D. 400, and perhaps a longer time. He shrank from publishing it to the last; and probably would not have done so when he did, and without further revision, had not the unfinished work been stolen and made public. The *De Civitate Dei* was begun in A.D. 413, and completed in A.D. 426. This has been generally regarded as his master-piece; and it is so well known that it does not need, any more than the *Confessiones*, any full analysis in this place. Presenting to his own age a bold and convincing apology for Christianity, it became to all ages the earliest philosophy of history; and in both aspects the work has high claim upon the grateful regard of mankind. Its range of thought is very wide; it comprises some of its author's most mature opinions upon topics of philosophy and theology; it anticipates many of the speculations of modern times.

A few words upon the *Retractationes* may complete our sketch of S. Augustine's literary labors. In this work, written in A.D. 427 or 428, he carefully reviews his previous writings, of course explaining former opinions by present ones, and, where possible, striving to bring the earlier views into harmony with the later. For him to have pursued any different course would not, it would seem, have been thought strange by some who have unduly criticised his criticism of himself.[1] We

---

[1] Neander's *Hist. of the Christian Religion and Church*, (Torrey's transl.) Vol. II. p. 694; Mozley's *Augustinian Doctrine*, etc. p. 360; Owen's *Evenings with the Skeptics*, Vol. II. p. 140.

leave to the bitterness of scepticism the rash implication that this aged saint had now lost all his comprehensiveness and Christian charity; and that the opinions he now rejected would make a better Christian creed than those he accepted.[1] He wrote of himself with a candor generally admitted; explaining, qualifying, and, where he thought necessary, contradicting what he had previously written and even admitting former opinions to have been downright errors. Thus much it is well for us to note just at this point; for even aside from special influences which we know had great weight in the latter part of his career, it was only natural that any one who had lived so long and written so much should have uttered contradictions. It is often said that S. Augustine can be quoted in favor of diametrically opposed doctrines. This is to a certain extent true, and for the reason which we have given. He had a deep humility. He thought a man to be "more a consummate fool than perfectly wise" of whom it could be said that he had never uttered a word which he did not wish to recall; that the highest standard was to have never uttered a word which it would be his *duty* to recall; and that he who had not attained to this, should take the second place through his humility, as he could not take the first through his wisdom.[2] Accordingly his estimate of himself (and let any prove that it was not the correct one) was that consistency was not of so much worth as *to have made progress*.[3] He says at this time that he

---

[1] Owen, *ut supra*.   [2] *Ep.* cxliii. 3.   A.D. 412.   [3] *Id.*.2. *De don persev.* 55.

is writing the *Retractationes* to demonstrate that even he himself has not in all things followed himself; admits that he did not begin from perfection, and has not yet in this age (74 years) reached perfection; and affirms that there is good hope of him whom the last day of life shall find so progressing, that whatever is wanting may be added, and that he may be adjudged rather to need perfecting than punishment.[1]

In A.D. 429 the Vandals under Genseric invaded Africa, at the invitation of Count Boniface, who had been deceived into rebellion against the Empire, and had summoned the barbarians to enable him to maintain himself. Discovering the treachery which had been practised against him, and returning to his allegiance, it was too late to save the country from the invaders. They readily made allies of the Donatists throughout the provinces, and fiercely pressed on in their career of conquest. Boniface retired to Hippo, and the city was besieged. In the third month, on the 28th of August, A.D. 430, the aged Bishop, who had been bitterly tried by the miseries of the times, and thought that men ought to ascribe Africa's calamities to their own sins, was mercifully taken away, after not a long illness. With the words of the Penitential Psalms written out and hung on the wall before his eyes, he had bade his friends leave him to himself as much as possible; and so he spent the last few days in solitude, and prayer, and tears. He died a penitent.

[1] *De don. persev.* 55.

In going on to a survey of the principal teaching of S. Augustine, we shall first follow the line of the three great controversies which have been referred to. He has very important and characteristic points of teaching which do not directly concern either of those controversies, though they may be found in part in the writings which they called out. Such doctrines we shall subsequently consider to some extent. At the outset we must say that we shall not aim at any treatment of S. Augustine's *philosophy* proper.

Manichaeism, of the writings against which we are first to speak, was a strange, eclectic system, founded upon the ancient Chaldaism, combining therewith Persian and (in the West especially) Christian elements. Its prominent mark was its absolute *dualism*. Teaching without compromise the two principles of good and evil, light and darkness, both of them eternal, and both eternally distinct, it practically taught two gods. From this dualistic beginning it developed a most fantastic mythology; while, connected with its weird fancies about creation and nature, it established an ethical theory of bald materialism, whereby the work of life was made to consist in the constant effort to separate the elements of light from the darkness; which meant, in actual morality, a greater or less degree of ascetic abstinence with no end beyond itself. The Manichaeans spurned Judaism, and equally spurned Catholic Christianity. Yet in the West they called themselves Christians, and their organization in some points faintly resembled that of the Christian Church. They rejected the Old Testament, and basely perverted the New; they held spurious dogmas of a Trinity, an Incarnation, and an Atonement; professing to believe in Christ, who was to them only a phantom, they took what they pleased of the teachings of Jesus and His Apostles, and with their own interpretation. The system proclaimed loud promises of knowledge and wisdom to all who were in search of truth, and professed to require nothing to be received which had not the proof of reason. Such permitted rationalism in belief, such inducement of "spiritual benefits on the basis of the religion of nature," had made Manichaeism widely popular in the West; and it was in North Africa that it gained its largest following.

Augustine, who had perhaps been won to the system chiefly by its plausible theory of the origin of evil, was delivered from it very much through its failure to satisfy his deeper questionings on this same subject. Now he set himself to oppose its many errors, with earnestness and confidence in the truth, and at the same time with a gentleness and meekness and desire to restore rather than to discomfit his adversaries which are worthy of note, as not only shown here, but as being the spirit which he uniformly maintained in controversy. "Let those treat you angrily," he says, "who know not the labor necessary to find the truth, and the amount of caution required to avoid error." . . . "Let those treat you angrily, who know not with what sighs and groans the least particle of the knowledge of God is obtained." . . . "Let neither of us assert that he has found truth," he exhorts; "let us seek it as if it were unknown to us both."[1]

The teachings of S. Augustine against Manichaeism relate principally to the Being of God, the nature of good, the nature and origin of evil, the freedom of the will, the authority of Scripture, the limits of reason and faith. Much of what he here says about God, and about evil, is also given more fully and in more direct connection with the hold which Manichaean error once had upon him, in the *Confessions*. GOD is the one, almighty Creator, infinite in goodness and power. He is spirit; not the material existence which Manichaeism fancied Him, with properties of extension into space;[2] yet a real Being, not an empty phantasm.[3] He is "the unchangeable Light," yet not "the corporeal brightness" which he once conceived Him to be, — "a bright and vast body, and [himself] a piece of that body."[4] "God is His own eternal happiness, . . . His own eternal light;"[5] . . . "the God we worship did not abide from eternity in darkness, but is Himself light, and in Him is no darkness at all; and in Himself dwells in light inaccessible; and the brightness of this light is His co-eternal wisdom."[6] God is unchangeable and incorruptible. "It cannot properly be said of the real substance of God that it has the choice of sinning or not sinning, for God's substance is absolutely unchangeable. God cannot sin, as He cannot destroy Himself."[7] God is the

---

[1] Con. Epis. Man. ii. iii. [2] *Conf.* iii. 7; *con. Epis. Man.* xv. xix.
[3] *Conf.* iv. 5, 7, &c. [4] *Conf.* iv. 2, 16; vii. 10. [5] *Con. Faust.* xxii. 9.
[6] *Id.* xxii. 21. [7] *Id.* xxii. 22.

chief good of all His creatures; for He is the supreme, the true *existence*.¹ "To reach God is happiness itself."² He is "the author of all natures;"³ hence, all natures, as such, are good; and it is the nature of good, that it is all from Him; while it is the nature of evil (negatively), that it is not from Him. Augustine goes farther than this, and sets forth now the teaching to which he always adhered, that *evil has no real existence*, — it is but the negation of existence. "There is no nature contrary to God. . . . You ask me, Whence is evil? I ask you in return, What is evil? . . . Evil is that which is contrary to nature; . . . Evil is *no nature*, if it is contrary to nature."⁴ Again, "The second kind of good is called a creature, which is liable to hurt through falling away. But of this falling away God is not the author, for He is the author of existence and of being. Here we see the proper use of the word evil; for it is correctly applied not to essence, but to *negation or loss*."⁵ "When the Catholic Church declares that God is the author of all natures and substances, those who understand this understand at the same time that God is not the author of evil. For how can He Who is the cause of the being of all things be at the same time the cause of their not being, that is, of their falling off from essence and tending to non-existence? For this is what reason plainly declares to be the definition of evil."⁶

Yet this which has no true existence, and is thereby

---

¹ *De Mor. Manich.* i. ² *De Mor. Eccles.* xi. ³ *Con. Epis. Man.* xxxiii. ⁴ *De Mor. Manich.* i. ii. ⁵ *De Mor. Manich.* iv. ⁶ *De Mor. Manich.* ii.

proved to be not from God, Augustine owns fills the heart with fear. (*Conf.* vii. 5.) "Whence is it?"—he once and again exclaims. Against the Manichaeans, who argued that they sinned from natural necessity,—it was not they, but the nature of darkness in them (*Conf.* vii. 3), he put the origin of sin and of evil in *the freedom of the will.* "There is no need" he says "of the origin of evil in an imaginary evil nature" (referring to the original *dualism* of this system), "since it is to be found in free-will. . . . The origin of sin is in the will; therefore in the will is also the origin of evil. . . . You take away the origin of evil from free-will, and place it in a fabulous nature of evil."[1] But what is that *free-will*, it may be asked, to which Augustine here refers? — that of man in his original state, or of man as fallen? Plainly the former:—and yet it is an open question whether he did not use the term, during all this period, both of the one condition and of the other. Because he writes, e.g. in certain connections in the *De Libero Arbitrio*, that he is speaking of that freedom in which man was created,[2] it has been perhaps too necessarily inferred that he must be always so understood in that treatise.[3] That he meant to represent this cause of sin as an original, self-determining power — whether before or after the Fall — is abundantly manifest. Witness such passages as these:—"Since the will is the cause of sin, and you ask the cause of that will; if I can discover this, will you not also seek the cause of this cause?

---

[1] *Con. Faust.* xxii. 22. [2] l. iii. c. 18. [3] Mozley's *Aug'n Doctr.* etc. p. 206.

And what limit of seeking can there be, what end of inquiry and discussion, — since you ought not to go beyond the root?"[1] "But what can be the cause of will, antecedent to will? For either there exists the will itself, and there is no going back of that root of will; or there is no will, and in that case no sin. Either, then, the will itself is the first cause of sinning, or no sin is that first cause."[2] Again, a true freedom, or power of choice, seems to be ascribed to man in his present state in the *De Duabus Animabus*. And what else but a true freedom in man fallen is implied in this passage? — He has been speaking of the angels as so created that they had the power of restraining their desires from the unlawful; and in not doing this, they sinned. "Great, then," he continues, "is the creature man, for *he is restored by this potentiality*, by which, if he had so chosen, he would not have fallen."[3] It is the same power which restores him that originally kept him. Whether S. Augustine afterwards came to deny free-will under the pressure of the Pelagian controversy, must be considered in its proper connection. But that he now maintained it, in its self-determining power, and found therein the only satisfactory cause of evil, as against the Manichaean notion of necessity, may perhaps be admitted, with but little, if any, qualification.[4]

What he says upon Holy Scripture, forms a very important part of S. Augustine's teaching at this period. In one of these treatises occurs his well known declara-

[1] *De Lib. Arbit.* iii. 48.   [2] *Id.* iii. 49.   [3] *Con. Faust.* xxii. 28.
[4] Cf. Neander, *ut sup.* Vol. II. p. 626.

tion, "I should not believe the gospel, except as moved by the authority of the Church,"[1] — wherein he openly affirms the true ground for the authority of Scripture, and takes a position from which there can be no alternative but the individualism which he charges against Faustus; — "Your design clearly is to deprive Scripture of all authority, and to make every man's mind the judge what passage of Scripture he is to approve of, and what to disapprove of."[2] These Manichaeans rejected the Old Testament, but professed to receive part of the New. S. Augustine defends the whole, as the Word of God,[3] handed down in the Church from the Apostles,[4] and exhibiting clear proofs of its claims in the extent of its conquest of the world.[5] He maintains the *oneness* of Scripture, and shows that where there are apparent contradictions, there is real harmony. This principle he urges, as between different portions of either the Old or the New Testament, and especially as between the Old and the New. One will stand or fall with the other. The Old Testament he considers as chiefly typical, in both conduct and precept; as foreshadowing the New, and particularly telling of Christ.

---

[1] *Con. Epis. Man.* v. It is amazing to find the objection actually raised by a clergyman of the Church (*Continuity of Christian Thought*, p. 150), that "the Church for which is claimed such supreme authority, is not the consentient reason of those who are enlightened by a divine teacher speaking within the soul"! — i.e. it is something different from that "human consciousness" which this writer regards as "the ultimate source of authority in religious truth" (pp. 17, 59, 60); but it *is* something *definite and visible*, the institution of God in the world.

[2] *Con. Faust.* xxxii. 19.   [3] *Id.* xxii. 16.   [4] *Id.* xi. 5.   [5] *Id.* xxii. 60.

"No one doubts," he writes, "that promises of temporal things are contained in the Old Testament, for which reason it is called the Old Testament; or that the kingdom of heaven and the promise of eternal life belong to the New Testament. But that in these temporal things were figures of future things which should be fulfilled in us upon whom the ends of the world are come, is not my fancy, but the judgment of the Apostle. . . . We receive the Old Testament, therefore, not in order to obtain the fulfilment of these promises, but to see in them predictions of the New Testament; for the Old bears witness to the New. . . . Nor do we believe that the holy and spiritual men of these times, the patriarchs and prophets, were taken up with temporal things. For they understood, by the revelation of the Spirit of God, what was suitable for that time, and how God appointed all these sayings and actions as types and predictions of the future. Their great desire was for the New Testament; but they had a personal duty to perform in these predictions, by which the new things of the future were foretold. So the life as well as the tongue of these men was prophetic."[1] This matter of symbolism and allegory S. Augustine often carried too far, as we know, in his interpretation of Scripture, especially of minute events in the historical books; only regretting, as he says again and again, that the length of his writing already will not permit him to go farther in his fine-spun analogies.[2] And yet, in his supreme regard for the *inner meaning* of Scripture, it

---

[1] *Id.* iv. 2; xxii. 24.   [2] *Id.* xxii. 86.

must be owned that he kept sight of the *literal sense*, — according to a general rule of interpretation among the Fathers;[1] here in his controversy against the Manichaeans, he examines the literal sense of each of these narratives "before he touches the sacramental or mysterious meaning;"[2] — furthermore, in that important writing *De Genesi contra Manichaeos* he takes a decided position against the allegorists; and then, several years later, in the *De Genesi ad literam*, he goes over the same ground speaking even more emphatically than before. But it is a constant principle with him that Scripture is to be interpreted *according to the analogy of the faith;* and so his final end in the investigation of lives and words of patriarchs and prophets is plainly *the figure,* —*the type.* "Every part of the narrative in the prophetical books" he says "should be viewed as having a figurative meaning, except what serves merely as a frame-work for the literal or figurative predictions."[3] He will not argue with those who will not take the narratives in this way: — "to dispute about such a difference of understanding would be as useless as to dispute about a difference of taste."[4] Moreover, he affirms that the typical or prophetical character of actions is not affected by their own moral quality. "In foretelling good, it is of no consequence whether the typical actions are good or bad. If it is written in red ink that the Ethiopians are black, or in black ink that

---

[1] Vid. Keble's *The Mysticism attributed to the Early Fathers*, p. 42; cf. Abp. Trench's *S. Augustine as an Interpreter* etc. p. 50 *et seq*.

[2] Keble, *ut sup.* p. 105.   [3] *Con. Faust.* xxii. 94.   [4] *Id.* xxii. 95.

the Gauls are white, this circumstance does not affect the information which the writing conveys. No doubt if it was a painting instead of a writing, the wrong color would be a fault; so, when human actions are represented for example or warning, much depends on whether they are good or bad; but when actions are related or recorded as types, the merit or demerit of the agents is a matter of no importance, so long as there is a true typical relation between the action and the thing signified."[1] This was one conclusive way which he had of explaining the morality of the Old Testament. The Manichaeans, either in reality or in pretence, made a great deal of the moral difficulties of all that part of the Bible, and sneered contemptuously at the character of the Old Testament saints. And in reply to them, besides this reference to actions and events as types, S. Augustine pressed strongly the principle of the Divine accommodation to the circumstances and moral standard of earlier ages, as justifying commands and permissions which in a later time would be wrong. He affirms that the true and good God, and He alone, could give such commands rightly;[2] that the order of time demanded such a dispensation;[3] and asks, "Do they not understand how precepts and counsels and permissions may be changed without any inconstancy in Him Who enjoins them, but by the wisdom of Him Who dispenses them according to the difference of the times?"[4] This progressive character of revelation, this gradual education of men into the knowledge of

[1] *Id.* xxii. 83.   [2] *Id.* xxii. 72.   [3] *Id.* xxii. 76.   [4] *Id.* xxii. 77.

God, as pointed out by the great Latin Father, is a topic which several writers have commented upon; and Canon Mozley has suggested that in this method of his he has indicated the true answer to objections of our own day against the morality of the Old Testament.[1] It is not the only instance in which his teaching meets the difficulties of modern thought.

The Manichaeans were rationalists; their system was one of rationalism; and much of what S. Augustine says against them upon the relations of reason and faith, might be wholesome medicine for the rationalism of our time. With him, having once accepted the authority of Scripture, it is a settled conviction to "believe because it is written."[2] He would not put understanding before faith, but faith before understanding. "Crede ut intelligas," was his bidding.[3] Yet he said truly that Catholic Christians "do not condemn the use of reason;"[4] only it must keep its proper relations, and act in its own sphere. He appears to have thought that in divine things it was not at first able to behold. "It falls back from the light of truth," he says; and then, by appointment of Divine wisdom, "we are met by the friendly shade of authority."[5] As he developed this idea, later in life, as given in one of his letters, it stood, — "The perfection of method in training disciples is, that those who are weak be encouraged to the utmost to enter the citadel of authority,

---

[1] *Ruling Ideas of Early Ages*, p. 272; and cf. Abp. Trench, *ut sup.* p. 40.
[2] *Con. Faust.* xxvi. 7.   [3] *Serm.* xliii. 3.   [4] *Con. Faust.* xviii. 7.
[5] *De Mor. Eccles.* vii.

in order that when they have been safely placed there, the conflict necessary for their defence may be maintained with the most strenuous use of reason. . . . Thus, the whole supremacy of authority and light of reason for regenerating and reforming the human race has been made to reside in the one saving Name, and in His one Church." [1] His treatise *De utilitate credendi*, which was written to help a friend out of the snares of Manichaeism, contains a clear and full presentation of this whole matter of the precedence of faith to reason. "If they say that we are not even to believe in Christ unless undoubted reason shall be given us, they are not Christians. For this is what certain pagans say against us, foolishly indeed, yet not contrary to or inconsistent with themselves. But who can endure that those profess to belong to Christ, who contend that they are to believe nothing unless they shall bring forward to fools most open reason concerning God? But we see that He Himself . . . willed nothing before, or more strongly than, that He should be believed in; whereas they with whom He had to do were not yet qualified to receive the secret things of God." [2] "It is authority alone," he says, "which moves fools to hasten unto wisdom. So long as we cannot understand pure truth, it would be indeed wretched to be deceived by authority, but surely more wretched not to be moved;" [3] — a passage which has been much abused, and made to teach what it does not teach. Surely all believers in the Church of Christ find in that Divine institution the meaning of

[1] *Ep.* cxviii. 32, 33. [2] *De util. credend.* 32. [3] *Id.* 34.

those other words, " We must not give up all hope that
. . . God Himself hath appointed some authority,
whereon resting, as on a sure step, we may be lifted up
unto God." [1] And because S. Augustine accepted authority, because he placed faith in order of time before
reason, there is no good ground for the charge of certain
recent writers, that he gave up his reason, and remained
ever more in blind and abject submission. We cannot
think that he regarded the authority which influenced
him to accept Christianity and the Church as "extrinsic
and separable from the truth of [that] Christianity." [2]
We find no proof that he considered "his volition
forced." [3] Nor need we admit the truth of such milder
language as that in "this earlier theology . . . he sufficiently satisfied his reason while yet making the sacrifice
of reason," [4] with its implication, — which the one who
writes these words fully confirms, — that in his later
thinking he made the sacrifice complete. That he became more dogmatic, and even grew in some ways more
narrow and fettered in his thinking, cannot be denied;
but, with all this, we find no ground for saying that he
more and more surrendered reason. On the other
hand, we believe that, in harmony with certain words of
his which we have quoted, he more and more *used reason*. He might hold, in such use, we claim, what ideas
he pleased, of free-will, or predestination; for the question of submission, which his opponents make so much
of, has not to do with the almighty and inscrutable

[1] *Id.* [2] Owen's *Evenings with the Skeptics*, Vol. II. p. 181. [3] *Id.* p. 182. [4] Allen's *Continuity of Christian Thought*, p. 148.

power of God, but with the authority of the Church, and of forms of truth, called dogmas.

It has been quite popular in modern times, to assert or to hint that S. Augustine was never free from the influence of Manichaeism. One says, "In spite of his war against the Manichaeans, he remained to the last unconsciously, but virtually and essentially Manichaean in his theory of human nature."[1] Another writes, "The real strength of Augustine was acquired, I conceive, through his early baptism in the Styx of Manichaeism, and his discovery that God must be the deliverer from it. I do not say that he ever shook off the distemper; it came back again frequently in his battle with Pelagius" etc.[2] But, admitting the unconscious influence which the apparent dualism of the universe may have continued to present to his mind, we cannot see the justice of any such charge. No one, we believe, who understands his doctrine of original sin, can truly affirm that by it human nature was annihilated, and made "only a medium for the manifestation of God or the devil."[3] Neander is more fair-minded. His statement is, that "Augustine's anthropological views have been *very unjustly* attributed to the influence of Manichaeism:"[4] — and he goes on to distinguish plainly his doctrine of human corruption, which "grew out of a simple fact of the moral consciousness," from the dualism of Mani's philosophy of nature. It was the Pelagians,

---

[1] Hedge's *Atheism in Philosophy and other Essays*, p. 188. [2] Maurice: — in his *Life* etc. Vol. II. p. 109. [3] Hedge, *ut sup.* p. 190. [4] *Ch. Hist.* Vol. II. p. 625.

chiefly, who used to taunt S. Augustine with being a Manichaean; and the reason was evident: perhaps the same reason moves those who cast the taunt now.

S. Augustine has left writings of much importance in connection with *Donatism*. This schism had been in existence in Africa from the beginning of the fourth century. Originating in false notions of the purity of the Church, it carried these notions to the extreme of bigotry and narrowness. Early calling out the opposition of the Empire, by refusing to yield to decisions given in answer to its own appeals, meeting henceforth with but little of conciliation, provoked by continued imperial repression, growing stronger by persecution, going to great lengths of gloomy zeal and even cruel fanaticism, the sect in Augustine's time had come to be one of large proportions and corresponding influence. The Donatists have been called the Puritans of Africa; and the history of the two presents many parallels, in doctrine and practice. S. Augustine, and the African Church quite generally, through his influence, made many efforts to win them back to the Church; and they succeeded to a good degree in certain sections; but the schism was too deep-seated, perhaps, in the very intensity of the African nature: it was but one of the forms of persistent dissension in that Church, which died only with the extinction of the Church itself. By letters, and treatises, and conferences, S. Augustine strove to bring the Donatists to their allegiance. While firm in his opposition to their error, he manifests a spirit of conciliation and courtesy and charity; he entreats his clergy and people to show "untiring gentleness." "Love men, while you destroy errors," are his words: — "take of the truth without pride; strive for the truth without cruelty; pray for those whom you refute and convince."[1]

His teaching in this connection relates to the validity and efficacy of the sacraments, especially Baptism; the purity of the Church; the unity of the Church; the sin of schism: — and what he writes upon these subjects is of permanent value. Nor would we fail to consider, in part for justification or explanation, in part for censure, his oft-quoted opinions about compulsion and persecution which were uttered at this time.

S. Augustine maintains the holiness and power of the Church's sacraments in language not to be misunderstood. They are holy, because they are Christ's sacraments; "holy, through Him to Whom they belong,"[2] and to Whom they unite those who worthily receive them. Their power is in Christ; and this power is for good or ill, according to the worthiness or unworthiness of the receiver. Speaking now of Holy Baptism, he writes, "He Himself consecrates His sacrament, — that in the recipient, either before he is baptized, or when he is baptized, or at some future time when he turns in truth to God, that very sacrament may be profitable to salvation, which, were he not to be converted, would be powerful to his destruction."[3] "When we say that Christ baptizes, we do not mean

[1] *Con. lit. Petil.* i. 31.   [2] *Con. lit. Petil.* ii. 88.   [3] *De Baptismo*, vi. 47.

by a visible ministry, . . . but by a hidden power in the Holy Spirit. . . . Nor has He now ceased to baptize; but He still does it, not by any ministry of the body, but by the invisible working of His majesty."[1] It is always Christ Who is here the origin, root, and head.[2] This holiness and power, moreover, are *inherent*, and depend not upon the giver or the receiver. "When baptism is given in the words of the gospel, however great the perverseness of him through whom, or of him to whom it is given, the sacrament is holy in itself, *on account of Him Whose sacrament it is.* And if any one, receiving it at the hands of a misguided man, yet does not receive the perversity of the minister, but only the holiness of the mystery, being closely bound to the unity of the Church in good faith and hope and charity, he receives remission of his sins, — not by the words, . . . but by the sacraments of the gospel flowing from a heavenly source. But if the recipient himself be misguided, on the one hand what is given is of no avail for the salvation of the misguided man; and yet, on the other hand that which is received remains holy in the recipient, and is not renewed to him if he be brought to the right way."[3] Farther still, this independent power of the sacrament pertains to it even when administered outside of the unity of the Church. Holy Baptism *belongs* to Christ, — *belongs* to His holy Church; and yet, S. Augustine teaches, it is found with those who are in heresy or schism. That he does not mean by this any bodies which have not valid orders, is plain

---

[1] *Con. lit. Petil.* iii. 59.   [2] *Id.* i. 6.   [3] *De Baptismo*, iv. 18.

from his own words at the very beginning of the *De Baptismo*, and from what we know of the history of these bodies, whose bishops possessed an actual consecration, however irregular and illegal, whereby "an Episcopal succession went on conferring holy orders."[1] His own words are, that "he who is ordained, if he depart from the unity of the Church, does not lose the sacrament of conferring baptism,"[2] which he possesses because he is ordained. Accordingly, those who have received this baptism in separation, if they return to the unity of the Church, are not to be re-baptized; for, he says, "we act rightly, who do not dare to repudiate God's sacraments, even when administered in schism."[3] This was meant to oppose the error of the Donatists, who, falsely claiming that the Church had not possessed pure orders since the time of their separation, would not receive any who came to them from the Church, without re-baptizing them. And so S. Augustine deduces the general principle of the *validity* of the sacrament in distinction from its *efficacy*, — its *character* in distinction from its *grace*. He says that the reason why S. Cyprian and those of his time took the ground they did in favor of re-baptizing, was "from their not distinguishing the sacrament from the effect or use of the sacrament;"[4] and again, — "if you say that the grace of baptism is identical with baptism, then it exists among heretics; but if baptism is the sacrament or outward sign of grace, while the grace itself is the

---

[1] *Vid. Ch. Quart. Rev.* Vol. XIX. p. 309.   [2] *De Baptismo*, i. 2.
[3] *Id.*   [4] *De Baptismo*, vi. 1.

abolition of sins, then the grace of baptism does not exist with heretics."[1] This grace, this remission of sins, constituting its true efficacy, he claims can be received only in unity with the Church. "Men may be baptized in communions severed from the Church, in which Christ's baptism is given and received; but it will only then be of avail for the remission of sins," when they are "reconciled to the unity of the Church."[2] Of the case of two, baptized without change of heart or life, one without and the other within the Church, "he is worse who is baptized without, — *because he is without;* for the evil of division is in itself far from insignificant or trivial."[3]

But let none imagine that S. Augustine did not go farther than any outward dividing lines, even when they bounded the divine organization. He taught the deep, spiritual unity with Christ in His Church: and he even went so far in this, that he is by many interpreted as believing in the theory of an invisible Church in this world.[4] He says in one place, "Nor is it those only that do not belong to it [the Church], who are openly guilty of the manifest sacrilege of schism, but also those, who, being outwardly joined to its unity, are yet separated by a life of sin":[5] and again, — "It does not follow that whosoever has the baptism of Christ is also certain of the remission of sins, if he has this only in the outward sign, and is not converted with a true

---

[1] *Id.* vii. 37. [2] *Id.* i. 18. [3] *Id.* iv. 23. [4] Vid. his explanation of S. John iii. 5, in *De Baptismo*, vi. 19; of S. Matt. vii. 24 etc. in 44, 45; and cf. *Con. lit. Petil.* ii. 178, 180, 247. [5] *De Bapt.* i. 14.

conversion of the heart."[1] As "the man who is baptized in heresy in the Name of the Holy Trinity does not become the temple of God unless he abandons his heresy;" so "the covetous man who has been baptized in the same Name, does not become the temple of God unless he abandons his covetousness which is idolatry."[2] Holiness of life he deems of cardinal importance, and dwells upon the gradual progressiveness of evil or of good in one's life. All this is quite enough to show that he did not make of Baptism that magic charm which some have taught he did. He goes even farther. Where recourse to baptism may not be had for want of time, he teaches that "faith and conversion of heart" may supply what is wanting:[3] though he does not say this to depreciate the sacrament, — as no one can intentionally do, who honors God, — but affirms, to the contrary, that no "perfection in the inner man" should induce one to "despise a sacrament which is applied to the body by the hands of the minister, but which is *God's own means for working spiritually a man's consecration to Himself.*"[4] That this means may accomplish its end, however, it must be used as God would have it, not in separation but in unity. Though all possess true baptism who have received it anywhere in the Name of the Holy Trinity, without deceit, and with some degree of faith,[5] what they thus have, in separation, is only the *character* of baptism, not its *grace.* Augustine insists that it is the sacrament, and

---

[1] *Id.* vi. 62. [2] *Id.* iv. 6. [3] *Id.* iv. 29. [4] *Id.* [5] *Id.* vii. 102; *Con. lit. Petil.* ii. 61.

therefore "should be acknowledged and revered;"[1] but that it is of no profit for remission and salvation outside the Church. Accordingly, he is quite consistent in bidding all who are without to return to unity. And however strict his doctrine may seem in its relation to all such; of however little benefit, it would appear, he must have regarded their baptism — stripped of grace; really their case was no worse in his mind than that of those baptized in the Church in insincerity. Either case was an abuse, a perversion of a divine gift; an unlawful use of a lawful privilege. God's grace was held in abeyance, he taught; just as, in the case of insincerity, is commonly taught to-day.

The *unity* for which he pleaded is thus shown to have been spiritual as well as external. It *was* external, organic, — handed down in succession from the Apostles, among whom he gave the primacy to S. Peter, while he explicitly claimed that his was not the only Episcopal chair; there must be unity also with S. James, and S. Cyprian; — with Jerusalem and Carthage, as well as with Rome;[2] — this organic unity any who were striving to sunder, were doing great wrong, and bringing sorrow to every loyal heart. "We behold with grief and lamentation peace broken, unity rent asunder, baptism administered a second time, and contempt poured on the sacraments, which are holy even when ministered and received by the wicked."[3] This is the root of the matter with S. Augustine, — that the sacraments,

[1] *De Baptismo*, iii. 13. [2] *Id.* ii. 2. *Con. lit. Petil.* ii. 118. [3] *Ep.* xliii. 24.

the unity, the authority, are Christ's. The unity of the Church is with him the deepest possible spiritual unity; not only a oneness of believer with believer, but the oneness of believers with Christ, and *in Christ*. Can any question the scriptural and reasonable grounds for this unity, as he here puts it? — "No one attains to salvation and eternal life who has not Christ for his Head. But no one can have Christ for a Head, who does not belong to His Body, which is the Church."[1] And the following statement guards with equal care both sides of the truth; — "The entire Christ is the Head and the Body; the Head is the Only begotten Son of God; the Body is the Church. He who agrees not with Scripture in the doctrine concerning the Head, although he may stand in external communion with the Church, notwithstanding belongs not to her. But he who holds fast to all that Scripture teaches concerning the Head, and yet cleaves not to the unity of the Church, belongs not to her."[2]

A few words more must be said at this point, about S. Augustine's opinion of S. Cyprian. Although Cyprian had taken the strong ground which has been referred to upon re-baptizing, yet he had shown a holy spirit of peace and charity, in not claiming that his opinions and those of his local Church at Carthage should bind others, and in not separating himself from their communion. S. Augustine nobly extols this peaceful spirit, and deems it of higher worth than knowledge of the mystery of the sacrament, *without charity*.[3] He justly

---

[1] *De Unitate Ecclesiae*, 49.   [2] *Id.* 7.   [3] *De Baptismo*, i. 28.

affirms, also, that S. Cyprian's authority, which the Donatists so loudly boasted of as on their side, was really against them, and in favor of the Church, because of his very tolerance and humility and determination to keep unity; while they were proud and intolerant, and vaunted forth the very extreme of the schismatical temper; although they had, besides, the decree of a council [1] against them, and so knew and transgressed a law of the Church which did not exist in Cyprian's day. It is worthy of note, — and the point has been wrought out by an able writer, [2] — how strongly *anti-papal* is the conception of Church authority which S. Augustine here presents. To a discerning mind he hardly appears, in this respect, as the great fore-runner of the domination of the papacy, as some seem to regard him. He praises S. Cyprian, because, while holding firmly his own opinions, and, in so doing, daring to utterly reject the authority of the Bishop of Rome, he would not make the point a condition of communion with others, as there was no universal Church authority in the matter. "No one of us,"—says S. Cyprian commended by S. Augustine,—"sets himself up as a bishop of bishops, or by tyrannical terror forces his colleagues to a necessity of obeying." [3] How radically different from all this have been the temper and action of the Roman Church, is too manifest to call for comment.

This unity of the Church, so important for building up Christ's kingdom in the world, S. Augustine main-

---

[1] Eighth canon of Arles. [2] In the *Church Quarterly Review*, vol. xvi. pp. 28-30. [3] *De Baptismo*, ii. 3.

tains may be kept without the sacrifice of *purity*. This is not saying that the Church is wholly pure in this world. Nor is it denying that, in its ideal, the Church is *holy in Christ*,[1] — that great truth of the Creed; but it is an admission of the actual condition of things, an attempt to explain it, and to better it. The Church on earth includes both good and bad; even as the net in the parable contains both good and bad fishes, or the field both wheat and tares. This primary conception of her condition has been represented as one which S. Augustine ingeniously made up and urged, merely as means of carrying his point against the Donatists, — as a lawyer holding a brief for the Church.[2] But such criticism is very far-fetched, brought even all the way from the one-sidedness of Donatist feeling, as may be read in the records of that time.[3] The application of one of the parables, it is to be observed, they could not deny; that of the other *S. Augustine did not invent, but rather S. Cyprian*.[4] In the Church, then, as it is on earth, S. Augustine teaches, to insist on finding absolute purity, or even that there can be no communion with the wicked, would be to destroy the Church. But, as it has continued to exist, its life must have been maintained, even in spite of its impurity. The good in it are not to sever themselves, and thus commit the sin of schism. "The good and faithful, certain of their own salvation, may continue to dwell in unity among

---

[1] This is Maurice's charge, — *Life*, etc. Vol. II. p. 167. [2] *Continuity of Christian Thought*, p. 152. [3] Vid. Neander, *ut sup*. Vol. II. p. 242. [4] Vid. Abp. Trench on *The Parables*, p. 91, n. 1.

the corrupt whom it is beyond their power to punish, seeking to root out the sin which is in their own heart."[1] We need not be partakers of other men's sins, by being in communion with them. What S. Paul forbids, he explains,[2] is consenting to these sins. Wicked men may be in the Church, partaking materially of the sacraments, while they do not belong to the Body of Christ:[3] yes, wicked men may administer these sacraments, whose holiness cannot even thus be polluted; God gives the Holy Spirit in the ministry of wicked men; but though *through* them, not *from* them; for the grace itself is only *from Himself*, or *through His saints.*[4] But this state of things is "not for eternity, but only for time; nor is it spiritual, but corporal." . . . "Let the separation in the body be waited for till the end of time, faithfully, patiently, bravely."[5] Let no one, he urges, give way to *individualism.* "Let no one say, 'I will follow such an one, — for he made me a Christian, he baptized me;'— let no one that preaches the Name of Christ, or administers the sacrament of Christ, be followed in opposition to *the unity of Christ.*"[6] The Church's ideal purity will appear hereafter. "On earth it includes both bad and good. On earth it loses none but the bad; into heaven it admits none but the good."[7] Thus does he present the great truths of the unity and the purity of the Church. With its organic structure handed down from the Incarnate

---

[1] *Con. Epis. Parmeniani*, iii. 12 et seq.   [2] *De Baptismo*, vii. 9.
[3] *Con. lit. Petil.* ii. 247.   [4] *De Bapt.* v. 28, 29.   [5] *Con. lit. Petil.* iii. 4.
[6] *l.l.* iii. 6.   [7] *Ep.* xliii. 27.

God, with its spiritual power its deepest, truest test, with *Christ alone sinless* its one source of grace and life, — may he not well say, "You are safe, who have God for your Father, and His Church for your mother"?[1]

S. Augustine has been much censured for his approval of compulsion in bringing men into the Church. He has been charged with favoring persecution; and has been even made responsible for the cruelties of the Inquisition. We reluctantly admit that there is some truth in all this; although we think his opponents have carried the matter, in certain directions, much too far. As regards the Donatists, it must be owned, in his favor, that his treatment of them for a long period was by methods of persuasion and argument; that he neither advocated nor permitted force; that he urged upon his clergy and people only peace and conciliation, — seeking to win a real victory over their narrowness and bigotry, and to gain them for the Church's unity rather than to transform them into hypocritical Catholics.[2] They, on the other hand, became increasingly violent and cruel, — their abominable conduct, as all history shows, far exceeding any thing charged against the Church. They went on, in their outrages, to the extent of most heinous crimes. It was *the State* that interfered, partly to carry out its laws against crime, partly to compel them to give up their property, to abandon their worship, and come into the Church. And here, as in all such cases since, there is a commingling of the temporal and the

---

[1] *Con. lit. Petil.* iii. 10. Compare the mis-statement of this passage in *Continuity of Christian Thought*, p. 152. [2] *Ep.* xciii. 17.

spiritual, in interests, rights, and duties. The question becomes, — how far S. Augustine called for, approved, sanctioned this compulsory interference of the State? He positively did approve it, he did ask for it : and it does not do away with this fact to know that, in the kindness of his own nature, he counselled, even implored lenity in the punishment of offenders.[1] He might have been justified in seeking for protection from the state against cruelty, violence, murder. The mad rage of fanaticism was aroused ; and he could see no other way of checking it than this. But he went on to make the great mistake of connecting questions of religious belief and worship with those of moral conduct, and to think compulsion right, yes, a good and wholesome thing, in reference to one as well as the other. Interpreting literally the language of the parable, "compel them to come in," — using the example of S. Paul, compelled to believe at his conversion, — " Why," he asked, " should not the Church compel her lost sons to return?"[2] At first he would not call it persecution, which he advocated, but "punishment," or "merciful correction;" but soon it was "truth persecuting falsehood," or "treachery chastised with the scourge of tribulation :"[3] later, it became the "righteous persecution which the Church of Christ inflicts upon the impious, in the spirit of love, that she may correct, and recall from error."[4] He made much reference to the wholesome effect of this persecution, — how that so many of the reformed Dona-

[1] *Ep.* cxxxiii. *ad Marcellinum.*   [2] *Ep.* clxxxv. 22, 23.   [3] *Con. lit. Petil.* ii. passim.   [4] *Ep.* clxxxv. 11.

tists were thankful that the imperial laws had been brought to bear against them and they had been rescued, even against their will.[1] He claims that kings are to serve the Lord, as kings, "by preventing and chastising with religious severity all acts done in opposition to the commandments of the Lord.[2] Sins against God are as amenable to human law as sins against men: — "Why," he openly asks, "when free-will is given by God to man, should adulteries be punished by the laws, and sacrilege allowed?"[3] The whole drift of this language is in one direction. And even when we make all fair allowance for sincerity of motive, and take into account his own mildness and gentleness of spirit, we can find little in his writings upon this subject which is not worthy of condemnation; and with sad surprise we wonder if he ever imagined the extent to which his opinions might be used and abused.

The Pelagian heresy called forth perhaps the most distinctive of S. Augustine's doctrinal teaching. The truths imperilled he considered were those of prime importance, the errors subtle and dangerous. The controversy was severe and long continued; and the fact that here, more than anywhere else in his writings, Augustine appears as *the Controversialist*, largely accounts for both the strength and the weakness of his statements.

Pelagianism, with a great deal that was true, in its origin and development, was mainly false in both. Its

[1] *Id.* 7, 13.   [2] *Id.* 19.   [3] *Id.* 20.

origin was in an exaggerated notion of human power and freedom, the development of which would logically do away with Christianity. It denied any inherited fault of our nature, and made sin only actual. It proclaimed the sufficiency of man for obeying God's commandments, and denied the necessity of direct supernatural grace. Gaining popular esteem by its appeal to the innate consciousness of freedom and responsibility, and by its successful use of that appeal in arousing indolent souls to effort in the ordinary duties of life; after all it could not be truly practical, but, "going upon ideas without considering facts," it made too little of actual human frailty and the power of evil habit, and so had no ability to meet those deeper needs which really existed, and for which Christianity would provide a remedy.

S. Augustine, whose overpowering sense of the sinfulness of man was but the echo of his own experience to the affirmations of Scripture; to whom, in idea, God's power was infinite, man's strength nothing, and so, God's grace indispensable to enable human weakness,—was alarmed from the first at the existence in the Christian Church of doctrines which he considered struck at the foundation of Christianity. *If* nature since the Fall had no infection, if we were born as pure and as free to obey God as was Adam before his disobedience, if man could and did really make the first beginning in turning to God, if the will were thus powerful, if there were no absolute need of internal Divine assistance, if the life could thus begin and continue acceptable, — *where was Christianity?* was it not practically useless? But conscience, experience, observation contradicted this, and confirmed the testimony of God's Word.

To enter upon any detailed history of the Pelagian controversy would be beyond the scope of this essay. It affected all Christendom: through its chief leaders, Augustine on the one side, Pelagius, Celestius, and Julian on the other, its doctrines, in their more or less extended application, came before many Bishops and Councils, and were approved or disapproved; the conclusion being that the Pelagian opinions were condemned by the Church in both East and West.[1] Of the issues of the controversy, and the consequent value of the Church's decision, we may form an opinion, if we will but consider, as Canon Bright says, "what effect e.g. the denial of real grace would have on the principle of sacraments; or what would be left of the practical religion of our Prayer-Book, after it had been revised in the interests of Pelagianism."[2]

The teachings of S. Augustine in this connection have been loudly praised and loudly blamed. We have for them, as a whole, neither praise nor blame unqualified. A distinction may be made among them. Some of these doctrines were not the novelties which they are mistakenly affirmed to have been; others, truly, were but the developments of his own thought from doctrines which had the authority of tradition.[3] Moreover, as a guide, in our estimate of them all, we may

---

[1] Carthage, A.D. 418: Third General Council, at Ephesus, A.D. 431.
[2] *Anti-Pelagian Treatises*, etc. Introd. p. xiv.   [3] *Id.* p. li.

readily observe that they tend to become increasingly *intense, unconditioned, arbitrary, one-sided.* And herein they illustrate a principle; for even, if we do not, as many would not, find mental difficulty in the *theory* of absolute predestination, or of irresistible grace, there is still this to be said, that, in the orderings of Divine providence, in the working of the will of God in the hearts of men, *there is another side of the truth.* It is this other side of the truth, which, in the intensity of some of his doctrinal statements relating to Pelagianism, he loses; and whether it arise from the pressure of controversy, or from continual meditation upon the one aspect of truth which seems to him most necessary, he thereby does present doctrine which is defective, imperfect, individualized, rather than whole, catholic, comprehensive. And it is just those portions of his doctrine which have been taken up and elaborated, pushed to farthest extremes, and perhaps given a really forced interpretation, by founders of sects; while the body of his teaching is the heritage and the blessing of the entire Church.

S. Augustine met the self-sufficiency of Pelagianism, in part, by his teaching concerning *original sin.* This doctrine the Pelagians denied; they held that our only connection with Adam's sin was in the imitation of it, and called Augustine's doctrine a novelty. But, while the precise expression may have originated with him,[1] the doctrine itself, he rightly claims, he did not devise, but it belonged to the Catholic faith from ancient

[1] *Ad Simplicianum*, i. 1.

times[1] and had been always guarded as part of that faith;[2] and in more than one of his treatises[3] he cites many of the Fathers of East and West as maintainers of it. The principal Scriptural authority to which he appeals is that of Rom. v. 12; where, in spite of the generally considered mistranslation of ἐφ' ᾧ, "in whom," — the *thought* of his doctrine, ("omnes ille unus homo fuerunt"[4]) is plainly contained in the πάντες ἥμαρτον. He had what he conceived to be an unanswerable practical argument in the universal custom of Infant Baptism in the Church:[5] and it is an insinuation which needs proof, that only from Augustine's time and because of his teaching in reference to original sin, Infant Baptism began to be the general practice.[6] The baptism of infants, he says, cannot be for remission of actual sins, — and yet, it is for remission of sin, — therefore it can be only for that of original sin. "Inasmuch as infants are not held bound by any sins of their actual life, it is the guilt of original sin which is healed in them by the grace of Him Who saves them by the laver of regeneration."[7] This *original sin*, he teaches, subjects all the unbaptized to condemnation; and accordingly they who so die are not believed to be saved. The most forbidding part of S. Augustine's teaching is that concerning the eternal punishment of the heathen, who had no opportunity, and of infants dying unbaptized.

[1] *De nupt. et concupisc.* ii. 25. [2] *De peccat. meritis*, iii. 14. [3] Especially in the *Con. Julianum.* [4] *De nupt.* etc. ii. 15. [5] *De pecc. mer.* etc. i. 39. Cf. *De Bapt. parvul.* i. 10. [6] *Continuity of Christian Thought*, p. 160. [7] *De pecc. mer.* etc. i. 24.

But what, more definitely, does he make this original sin to be? It is that taint, or defect, or flaw[1] which our nature inherits from Adam. "We are in such a condition, because, by reason of his preceding sin, we are born in sinful flesh."[2] He, the head of the race, having disobeyed, and thereby incurred guilt, has, by the very law of transmission, made his descendants sharers in that guilt.[3] And it is *even more* than a law of transmission which is in exercise; for Adam was the divinely appointed head of the race, in whom the race was on trial. As he says elsewhere, — "We all were in that one man, for we all *were* that one man."[4] This original sin need not mean a literal imputation of Adam's sins to us, although some have so interpreted Augustine's teaching; but a condition which, by inheritance, brings to us the consequences of his act from whom we inherit. "Through the sin of the first man, which issued from his free-will, our nature became vitiated and ruined; and nothing ever came to its succor but God's grace alone, through Him Who is the Mediator," etc.[5] Again, "Having been born after Adam in the flesh, they have contracted, from

---

[1] *De nupt.* etc. ii. 49. [2] *De pecc. merit.* i. 68.

[3] In considering this law of descent by natural generation, Augustine enters upon the question of the origin of the soul, whether according to *traducianism* transmitted from parents to children, or according to *creatianism* by individual creation at each birth. He cannot decide in favor of either, and thinks the question not important, but inclines towards the latter, — one of many instances showing his candor, as the other theory would more manifestly agree with his doctrine.

[4] *De Civ. Dei*, xiii. 14.   [5] *De Grat. Chr.* i. 55.

their very birth, the contagion of the primeval death."[1] These passages are specimens of very many which exist in his works, and perhaps they show sufficiently what he believed original sin to be.

Certain inquiries suggest themselves. As to *the source* of this evil which we necessarily inherit,— is God made the Author of it? S. Augustine emphatically says, No. Human *nature*, as created in Adam, was good. Our *nature*, as such, has no evil in it. Adam possessed, in that nature, a perfect righteousness, the gift of supernatural grace, and this by supernatural grace he might have retained.[2] When he sinned, it was by his own free-will, and accordingly of this sin God must not be made the author. Evil thus arose *out of* good, it must be owned; as originally it did when a holy angel became the devil; but God was not its author. It sprang not from the supreme good which is His nature, but from that good which He created out of nothing.[3] Nor did Augustine thereby take refuge in Manichaeism; for the devil was not an original principle of evil, but was at first a good nature, made by the one good God. Another inquiry arises, as to *the extent* of this evil of original sin. He says our nature became "vitiated and ruined;" but, strong as this language is, or any other that can be quoted from him on this topic, we cannot discover it to be his teaching that thereby "the traces of the divine image in human nature were destroyed;" or that "hu-

---

[1] *De pecc. merit.* iii. 10.   [2] *De corrept. et grat.* 31.   [3] *De nupt.* etc. ii. 48, 50.

manity is absolutely separated from God."[1] Let us read what he says:—"God's image has not been so completely erased in the soul of man by the stain of earthly affections, as to have left remaining there no merest lineaments of it." . . . "What was impressed on their hearts when they were created in the image of God, *has not been wholly blotted out.*"[2] Again, "the blessing" [of creation]—(*creation* then is *a blessing*)—"has not been eliminated out of our excellent nature by a fault which puts us under condemnation. . . . Whatever sins men commit," (and certainly actual sins are worse than original sin)—"these *defects of character* do not eliminate his manhood from man; nay, God's good workmanship continues still, however evil be the deeds of the impious."[3] In the *De Trinitate*, (and in one of the closing books, which accordingly must have been written at the very time when he was in the heat of the Pelagian controversy,) he has very explicit words about the image of God in man, claiming that "this image, however worn out and defaced, still remains;" moreover, this "weak and erring mind, by this image of God within itself has such power as to be able to cleave to Him Whose image it is, to understand and behold God;"[4]—words by which he did not intend to deny the need of God's grace, but which show how highly he regarded human freedom *under* Divine grace, even in the initiative act of turning to God. Furthermore, if

---

[1] *Continuity of Christian Thought*, p. 157. [2] *De Sp. et lit.* 48.
[3] *De pecc. orig.* ii. 46. [4] *De Trin.* xiv. 6, 11, 20.

in his teaching of original sin, "humanity is absolutely separated from God," where could he have thought there would be *any point of contact or recovery* for our race, any more than for the fallen angels? And so the one who makes this statement can justify it only by the further assertion that Augustine is so deeply interested in establishing his position of the condemnation of the race, that "the redemption of the world by Christ inevitably assumes a subordinate place, and is practically denied;"[1] — that he is guilty of such "depreciation of Christ, that deism is the tacit assumption of the Church on which its institutions rest."[2] S. Augustine denying the redemption of Christ! S. Augustine *a deist!* Such an attack needs no defence but to ask all to read his writings with unprejudiced mind.

In the depth of the ruin which he believed the sin of Adam had brought upon the race, he never fails to recognize the mercy of God, following after man with every inducement of fear and of love, to bid him return to Him and be saved. But man has no power of himself to return. Not only has he no merit, whereby he can please God in doing good works, but he cannot *begin* to believe and obey, of himself. He must have this internal, supernatural power imparted, to inspire, to urge, to aid. It must "prevent and follow" him; it must be constantly with him. And this power is *Grace*, in the Augustinian teaching. Shall any one presume to say, that there is here a "degradation of Christian theology?" — that "Christ . . . gives way, in

[1] *Continuity of Christian Thought*, p. 157.   [2] *Id.* p. 171.

the system of Augustine, to an impersonal thing or substance which is known as grace?"[1] Where, then, we ask, is the presence of Christ in the inspired teaching of S. Paul? Is "grace" *there* only "an impersonal thing or substance," whose idea is to displace Christ in the heart? Grace is, indeed, a theological term; but its meaning reaches much farther than to the dry shell of dogma which sceptics and semi-sceptics talk about. It has been well defined, as "a force in the spiritual order, — not simply God's unmerited kindness in the abstract, but such kindness in action, as a movement of His Spirit within the soul, *resulting from the Incarnation*, and imparting to the will and the affections a new capacity of obedience and love."[2] And this it is in S. Augustine's teaching, herein carefully agreeing with Scripture and tradition.

The Pelagians were willing to call by that term the powers of nature originally conferred on man, and which, they taught, he had still in exercise; or they might make it another expression for the moral law, or the gift of forgiveness, or the following of Christ's example. And so they had a great deal of use, more or less specious, of the word *grace*. But they never came to own it as that internal, Divine power, which was necessary for holiness. Accordingly they and S. Augustine were not speaking of the same thing at all; and he is careful to say so repeatedly. He means by it that merciful power of God acting to restore man's fallen nature. Grace does not really disparage nature, he

---

[1] *Continuity* etc. p. 162. [2] Canon Bright's *Introduction, ut sup.* p. x.

says: — it "liberates and controls nature;"[1] it is not according to merit, or it would not be grace; it is free, or it would not be grace; it is set in contrast to the law, yet it enables to keep the law; grace works with us as well as in us; with our will, — establishing free-will; all grace is *in Christ*, by Whom it is given in many ways, emphatically in the Holy Sacraments; grace gradually accomplishes perfection in holiness, and brings us to the fruition of everlasting life. Our grace, he teaches, is an even greater gift than that bestowed upon Adam; for ours is efficacious, — yes, as he *may* be interpreted, even irresistible and indefectible. And now, if we add the relation of predestination and perseverance, in his system of doctrine, to this grace, — that predestination prepares for grace; and that this grace, by God's righteous and secret counsels, is not given to all alike, in fact *is* given to one and *not* given to another, for some never begin, and some do not finish the Christian course, — perhaps we shall have traced a tolerably clear outline of the Augustinian teaching on this great subject. Even in its outline it indicates bright lights and deep shadows; a mixture of Catholic truth and individual error; the error being in going so far with one side of truth as not to make known the other side; in being driven on by logic; in ignoring comprehensiveness, and being bound to a system; in forgetting authority, and making an excessive use of human reason. A few quotations may best illustrate all this. — "This grace of Christ . . . is not bestowed for any merits, but is given *freely*,

---

[1] *Retract.* ii. 43.

on account of which it is also called *grace*."[1] "The law was given in order that grace might be sought; grace was given in order that the law might be fulfilled."[2] "Does not the whole scope amount to this, that the letter which forbids sin fails to give man life, but rather killeth by increasing concupiscence and aggravating our sinfulness by transgression, unless indeed grace liberates us by the law of faith which is in Christ Jesus, when His love is 'shed abroad in our hearts by the Holy Ghost which is given to us'?"[3] "It is grace which helps any man to be a doer of the law; and without this grace, he who places himself under the law will be a hearer of the law and nothing else."[4] "God is said to be *our Helper;* but nobody can be *helped* who does not make some effort of his own accord. For God does not work our salvation in us as if we were mere stones, without sensibility, or creatures in whose nature He had placed neither reason nor will. Why, however, He helps one man, but not another, or why one man so much, and another not to the same extent, or why one man in one way, and another in another way, — are points which He reserves to Himself according to the method of His own most secret judgment, and to the excellency of His power."[5] "No man is assisted [by God], unless he also himself does something; assisted, however, he is, if he prays, if he believes, if he is 'called according to God's purpose.'" . . . "This God's grace does, in coöperation with ourselves, through Jesus

---

[1] *De nat. et grat.* 4. [2] *De Sp. et lit.* 34. [3] *Id.* 25. [4] *De grat. et lib. arbit.* 24. [5] *De pecc. merit.* ii. 6.

Christ our Lord, as well by commandments, sacraments, examples, as by His Holy Spirit also, through Whom there is *latently* shed abroad in our hearts that love which maketh intercession for us with groanings that cannot be uttered, until health and salvation be perfected in us, and God be manifested to us as He will be seen in His eternal truth."[1] "He begins His influence by working *in us* that we may have the will, and completes it by working *with us* when we have the will"[2] (the language of our Tenth Article). "Every man's righteousness must be attributed to the operation of God, although not taking place without the coöperation of man's will."[3] "Our merits have their crown of reward; but our merits are the gift of God;"[4] — the same sentiment as is found in the well known prayer of the *Confessions*, "Give what Thou commandest, and command what Thou wilt" (x. 40), or in the acknowledgment, "My good deeds are Thy institutions and Thy gifts" (x. 5), or in the Epistle to Sextus, "When God crowns our merits, He only crowns His own gifts."[5] "Do we by grace make void man's *freedom of will?* God forbid! We rather establish that faculty. For as the law is not weakened or cancelled by faith, neither is free-will by grace."[6] "If there is no grace of God, how does He save the world? and if there is no free-will, how does He judge the world?"[7] "By faith comes the acquisition of grace to resist sin; by grace the soul

---

[1] *De perfec. justit.* 43. [2] *De Grat. et lib. arbit.* 33. [3] *De Spir. et lit.* 7. [4] *De gest. Pelag.* 35. [5] *Ep.* cxciv. 19. [6] *De Spir. et lit.* 52. [7] *Ep.* ccxiv. 2.

procures healing from the disease of sin; by the health of the soul liberty is given to the will; from this freedom of the will arises the love of righteousness; and from the love of righteousness proceeds the accomplishment of the law. . . . How is it, then, that miserable men dare to be proud, either of their free-will, before they have liberty, or of their own strength, if they have been liberated?"[1] This grace is all *in Christ, and from Him.* This Mediator, "even previous to His coming in the flesh, all along delivered the ancient members of His Body by their faith in His incarnation;"[2] and "without faith in His incarnation, and death, and resurrection, the Christian verity unhesitatingly declares that the ancient saints could not possibly have been cleansed from sin, so as to have become holy, and justified by the grace of God."[3] "If God willed not that man should be without sin, He would not have sent His Son, without sin, to heal men of their sins."[4] "There is no reconciliation except by the remission of sins, through the grace alone of the most merciful Saviour, — through the only sacrifice of the most veritable Priest."[5] "In Him Who is our Head [is] the very fountain of grace, whence, according to the measure of every man, He diffuses Himself through all His members. It is by that grace that every man from the beginning of his faith becomes a Christian, by which grace that one Man from *His* beginning became *Christ;* the former also is born again *by the same Spirit* of which the latter was born."[6]

[1] *De Spir. et lit.* 52.   [2] *De pecc. orig.* 37.   [3] *De pecc. orig.* 28.
[4] *De perfec. justit.* 7.   [5] *De pecc. merit.* i. 56.   [6] *De praedest. sanct.* 13.

"The very sacraments of the holy Church show plainly enough that infants . . . are delivered from the bondage of the devil through the grace of Christ." [1] "Through the grace of that holy laver which we have put within our reach, advances are even now made by us towards the blessed consummation of perfection." [2] Although absolute perfection (he believed) might be, in theory, possible, — and "it must not by any means be said that with God there is no possibility whereby the will of man can be assisted to such a degree, that there can be accomplished in every respect, even now, in a man, not that righteousness only which is of faith, but that also in accordance with which we shall by and by have to live for ever in the very vision of God;" — yet, they who ask why this is not actually so now, forget "the fact that they are human."[3] "There is now a training carried on in growing [Christians], and there will be by all means a completion made, after the conflict with death is spent."[4] "The same regeneration which now sanctifies even our outer man,[5] and renews our spirit, so that all our past sins are remitted, will by and by also operate, as might be expected, to the renewal to eternal life of that very flesh."[6] "By this laver of regeneration and word of sanctification all the evils of regenerate men of whatever kind are cleansed and healed, — not the sins only which are all now remitted in baptism, but those also which after baptism are committed by human

---

[1] *De pecc. orig.* 45.   [2] *De pecc. orig.* 44.   [3] *De Spir. et lit.* 66.
[4] *De perfec. justit.* 16.   [5] *De nupt. et concupis.* i. 20.   [6] *De pecc. orig.* 44.

ignorance and frailty;" '—i.e. (as he more fully declares) "not only all the sins, but all the ills of men of whatever kind so ever, are *in course of removal* by the sanctification of that Christian laver whereby Christ cleanses His Church."[2] And this grace of Baptism is accompanied by that of the Eucharist; and even to infants is *this further grace* given; for, although S. Augustine seems to teach in some places that their incorporation into Christ is enough to make them partakers of His Body and Blood, the receiving of the Eucharist also is made generally necessary, (and herein he only follows the teaching of the Greek Church) in such passages as this,—"Reconciliation through Christ is in the laver of regeneration, and in the Flesh and Blood of Christ, without which not even infants can have life in themselves."[3]——"Did not Adam," asks S. Augustine, "have the grace of God? Yes, truly, he had it largely, but of a different kind. He was placed in the midst of benefits which he had received from the goodness of his Creator; for he had not procured those benefits by his own deservings; in which benefits he suffered absolutely no evil."[4] "God did not will even him to be without His grace, which He left in his free-choice.... Such was the nature of the aid, that he could forsake it when he would, and could continue in it when he would: but not such that he could be *made*

---

[1] *De nupt.* etc. i. 38.   [2] *Id.* 39.

[3] *Con. duas literas* etc. iv. 8. Cf. ii. 7, and iv. 4. The fuller reference to S. Augustine's teaching concerning the grace of the Eucharist, as given in other writings, is reserved for a distinct topic.

[4] *De correp. et grat.* 29.

to will his continuance. This first is the grace which was given to the first Adam; but more powerful than this is that in the second Adam. For the first is that whereby it is effected that a man may have righteousness if he will; the second can do more than this, since by it it is even effected *that he will,* and wills so much, and loves with such ardor, that by the will of the Spirit he overcomes the will of the flesh."[1] "To the first man . . . was given the aid of perseverance; not that by it it might come to pass that he should persevere, but because without it he could not of free-will persevere. But now, to the saints predestinated by God's grace, . . . it is not only that without that gift they cannot persevere, but . . . that by means of this gift *they cannot help persevering.*"[2] So he concludes "therefore aid was brought to the infirmity of human will, so that it might be *unchangeably and invincibly influenced* by Divine grace; and thus, although weak, it still might not fail, nor *be overcome by any adversity.*"[3] — "God's predestination in good is the preparation of grace; which grace is actually the endowment itself, — the effect of that very predestination."[4] "'But why,' says one, 'is not the grace of God given according to man's merits?' I answer, 'Because God is merciful.' 'Why, then,' it is asked, 'is it not given to all?' And here I reply, 'Because God is a Judge.' And thus grace is given by Him freely; and by His righteous judgment it is shown in some, what grace confers on those to whom it is given."[5]

---

[1] *Id.* 31. [2] *Id.* 34. [3] *Id.* 38. [4] *De praedest. sanct.* 19.
[5] *De don. persev.* 16.

"If you ask, 'Why will He punish me rather than another, or deliver him rather than me?' I confess that I can find no answer to make."[1] "Is there unrighteousness with God? Away with the thought! But His ways are past finding out. Therefore let us believe in His mercy in the case of those who are delivered, and in His truth in the case of those who are punished, without any hesitation; and let us not endeavor to look into that which is inscrutable, nor to trace that which cannot be found out."[2] "From all which it is shown with sufficient clearness that *the grace of God*, which both begins a man's faith and enables it to persevere, *is not given in respect of our merits*, but according to His own most secret, and at the same time most righteous, wise, and beneficent will. . . . We therefore will, but God worketh in us to will also. We therefore work, but God worketh in us to work also for His good pleasure."[3]

The question of *free-will* is strictly a philosophical one; yet, as it is presented in S. Augustine's teachings, it has so important a relation to other questions, that, while we do not profess to enter into it with any degree of minuteness, we are not permitted to pass it by. *Did S. Augustine teach free-will?* Yes; *absolutely, in reference to man before the Fall*. This teaching comes out clearly in his earlier writings, wherein, as we have already hinted, we think it quite probable that he also meant to teach this absolute freedom in man fallen. But in these later works,—emphatically in the Anti-

---

[1] *De don. persev.* 18.   [2] *Id.* 25.   [3] *Id.* 33.

Pelagian writings, under the pressure of controversy, he certainly propounds a different theory in reference to the present condition of the race. Some have ventured to call this teaching that of a genuine freedom. Poujoulat affirms that Augustine teaches the Catholic doctrine to be "not at all the destruction of free-will, but its profound modification;" and says, "so far is free-will from being destroyed in sinful man [according to Augustine], it is this free-will which *determines his sinfulness*,"[1] a statement which does not go very deep. Many other Roman Catholic writers have strongly maintained a similar position, and upon like grounds, — notably, perhaps, a thoughtful critic of Canon Mozley's *Augustinian Doctrine of Predestination*, in the fortieth volume of the *Dublin Review*. Julius Müller, in his *Christian Doctrine of Sin*, distinguishes a three-fold sense of S. Augustine's use of the term *freedom*, — (1) that of *absolute power of choice* between good and evil, as belonging originally to the first man; (2) that *spontaneity* essentially belonging to the human will, which marks man's present condition; wherein, though he be under the power of necessity, he is free from constraint; and (3) that *highest freedom*, which, beginning in the present condition, by the power of grace, can be perfect only in the future life, *when it will be impossible to sin*.[2] Canon Mozley, in the work above referred to, very fully treats of Free-Will as held by S. Augustine to belong to fallen man; and concludes,

---

[1] *Histoire de S. Augustin*, III. p. 125.   [2] Vol. II. p. 35. (Edinb. translation.)

by much reasoning, and from many references, that it means only the possession of *a will;* that in part it does not come up to the received doctrine of free-will, — the will as a self-determining power, — and in part opposes it.[1]

We have already given several passages in which S. Augustine speaks of free-will in its relations to *grace.* His teaching may further appear in what follows. His theory, in few words, is this, — that through the Fall man lost his primal liberty and the grace which bestowed it: he is accordingly free only in the direction of sin, until the grace of Christ sets him free. And yet he may have this grace always, in answer to prayer, and in ordinances of the Church; so human responsibility is guarded, while his own consciousness of *practical freedom* is answer enough to the insinuations of fatalism. That such a theory teaches the *libertas indifferentiae* can hardly be averred; that it may be a higher and truer theory cannot be denied. "Which of us can say," he writes, "that by the sin of the first man free-will perished from the human race? Through sin *liberty* indeed perished, but it was that liberty which was in Paradise, — of having *a full righteousness with immortality*, on account of which loss human nature is without divine grace." . . . But "free-will did not so far perish in the sinner but that by it all sin; . . . *they will what pleases them*. Whence also the Apostle says, 'When ye were the servants of sin, ye were free from righteousness.' . . . They are not, then, free from right-

[1] pp. 195-232, (third edition.)

eousness except by the choice of the will, but they do not become free from sin save by the grace of the Saviour."[1] He puts very strongly the necessity which "a penal viciousness produced out of the original liberty." "Vanquished by the sin into which it fell by the bent of its will, *nature has lost its liberty*. . . . Because the will turned to sinning, the hard necessity of possessing sin pursued the sinner."[2] So now "the captive will cannot breathe into a wholesome liberty save by God's grace."[3] Free-will "is of force for sinning in men subjected to the devil; while it is not of avail for pious living, unless made free by God's grace."[4] Accordingly, "he who falls, falls by his own will, and he who stands, stands by God's will."[5] Grace "changes the will from bad to good, and assists it when good."[6] Yet "it is not to be for a moment supposed, because S. Paul said 'it is God that worketh in you' etc., that he meant to do away with the liberty of the will. If this had been his meaning, he would not have said just before, 'Work out your own salvation'" etc.[7] "What need for further question?" he writes, "since we call that *power*, where to *the will* is joined the ability *to do*. That is in a man's power, which he does if he wills, and if he does not will, does not do."[8] (*Quod si*

---

[1] *Con. duas literas*, etc. i. 5.

[2] *De perfec. justit.* 9. *Cf.* the strong language in the *Enchiridion*, xxx. — "It was by the evil use of his free-will that man destroyed both it and himself."

[3] *Con. duas literas*, etc. iv. 3.   [4] *Id.* ii. 9.   [5] *De don. persev.* 19.   [6] *De grat. et lib. arbit.* 41.   [7] *Id.* 21.   [8] *De Spir. et lit.* 53.

vult, facit, si non vult, non facit.) Again, — "what is believing, but agreeing to the truth of what is asserted? But consent proves the possession of will, (*volentis est;*) — *faith, therefore, is in our own power.*"[1] "To yield our consent, or to withhold it, . . . is the function of our own will."[2] And this is true, he says, however much God influence us, externally or internally. Prayer, too, proves resistance to sin *possible.* "Whatever may be the cause [of sin], it may be resisted. Plainly it may. For on this account we pray for help, saying 'Lead us not into temptation.' This help we should not ask, if we believed that resistance were quite impossible."[3] So S. Augustine would bring his readers to the conclusion that the Pelagians "do not maintain free-will by purifying it, but demolish it by exaggerating it."[4] The practical question is, "What the ability of man's will can do, when assisted by the grace of God."[5] And here, God does not command *impossibilities.* "Nor is any one," he says, "forced by God's power *unwillingly,* either into evil or good; but when God forsakes a man, he deservedly goes to evil, and when God assists, without deserving he is converted to good. For a man is not good if he is *unwilling,* but by the grace of God he is even assisted *to the point of being willing.*"[6] "Who is drawn, if he was already willing? And yet no man comes unless he is willing. Therefore he is drawn in wondrous ways *to will,* by

---

[1] *De Spir. et lit.* 54. [2] *Id.* 60. [3] *De. nat. et grat.* 80. [4] *Con. duas literas* etc. i. 8. [5] *De nat. et grat.* 49. [6] *Con. duas literas* etc. i. 36.

Him Who knows how to work within the very hearts of men."[1]

The last two complete treatises of S. Augustine, in this great controversy, have to do with *Predestination* and *Perseverance*. Election is of God's mercy, he teaches; and God's ways are unsearchable. Nor is it any contradiction, "that grace is exceedingly secret."[2] God "has mercy, when He gives good things. He hardens, when He recompenses what is deserved."[3] Predestination is but a particularizing of God's foreknowledge.[4] "This is the predestination of the saints, — nothing else; viz. *the foreknowledge and the preparation of God's kindnesses*, whereby they are most certainly delivered, whoever they are that are delivered."[5] Our Lord, in His Incarnation, he regards as the grandest instance of predestination. It was "that same predestination of the saints which most especially shone forth in [Him] *the Saint of saints*."[6] This predestination is absolute. God chooses men *that they may be* believers, not because *they are already so*,[7] nor because *He foresees they will be so:*[8] nor is any one to be judged according to what he might have done, if he had lived longer.[9] The statement grows even more intense: "it did not do [the Jews] any good that they were *able to believe*, because they were not *predestinated* by Him Whose judgments are inscrutable, and His ways past finding out. Neither would it have been a hindrance to them that

---

[1] *Con. duas literas* etc. i. 37. [2] *De praedest. sanct.* 13. [3] *Id.* 14.
[4] *Id.* 19. *De don. persev.* 41. [5] *De don. persev.* 15, 35. [6] *De praedest. sanct.* 31. [7] *Id.* 34. [8] *Id.* 37. [9] *Id.* 24.

they *could not believe*, if they had been so predestinated, as that God should illumine their blind eyes"[1] etc. And "if, on the hearing of this, some should be turned to torpor and sloth, and from striving, should go headlong to lust after their own desires, is it therefore to be accounted that what has been said about the foreknowledge of God is false?"[2] It was at this period that he could allow himself to interpret "Who will have all men to be saved" (1 Tim. ii. 4), as meaning only that "no man is saved unless God wills his salvation;"[3] — "all men" meaning "all classes of men," or "every race of men." —— We are to pray for *perseverance*, for ourselves and others, — for it is God's gift. The Lord's prayer, he explains, is pre-eminently the saints' prayer for perseverance.[4] Even they who do not persevere may have been *receivers of grace*. Those, he says, "must be called Christ's disciples and God's children, whom, *being regenerated*, we see to live piously; but they *are then truly* what they are called, if they shall abide in that on account of which they are so called."[5] Predestination "must be preached," for it bids men glory in the Lord; and it need not discourage, any more than preaching God's gifts need discourage obedience.[6] Yet, it is to be proclaimed *with great discretion*, implying need of action, and the reward promised, and making general application of the truth, and speaking to all present as if they might be receivers of grace.[7] And,

---

[1] *De don. persev.* 35. [2] *Id.* 38. [3] *Enchirid.* ciii. Cf. *De correp. et grat.* 44. [4] *De don. persev.* 3. [5] *De correp. et grat.* 22. [6] *De don. persev.* 50, 51. [7] *Id.* 57–61.

as no one can be certain of eternal life until death, he again more strenuously urges the duty of prayer.[1] —— We may not pass over his allusion, in one of the closing chapters of the treatise *De dono perseverantiae*, to the pressure which the controversy has brought to bear upon him, — how that *necessity* has compelled him to "more carefully and laboriously defend the sacred Scriptures, because of these special heresies." For "the Pelagians say that God's grace is given according to our merits; and what else is this than an absolute denial of grace?"[2]

In all these writings of S. Augustine perhaps the greater part of his reasoning may be admitted, and that too without calling it "the seductive glamour of his dialectic,"[3] which is going to ensnare us and captivate us : and if we own that great principle of *the other side of truth*, most of his conclusions upon these majestic themes need not surprise us, if we are thinking people, who have ever met speculative difficulties. To some there may be help towards the balancing of the Divine and the human relations of these deep mysteries in his own words in the *De Civitate Dei*,— words more calm and quiet and spiritually devout, more like himself. "It does not follow, that, though there is for God a certain order of all causes, there must therefore be nothing depending on the free exercise of our own wills, for *our wills themselves are included in that order of causes which is certain to God, and is embraced by His foreknowledge,* — for human wills are also causes

---

[1] *Id.* 62, 63. [2] *Id.* 53. [3] Owen.

of human actions; and He Who foreknew all the causes of things would certainly among those causes not have been ignorant of our wills." . . . "Neither let us be afraid, lest, after all, we do not do by will that which we do by will, because He Whose foreknowledge is infallible foreknew that we would do it."[1] We need not "have any dread of *necessity* taking away the freedom of our will." . . . "We are by no means compelled, retaining the prescience of God, to take away the freedom of the will, or retaining the freedom of the will, to deny that He is prescient of future things, which is impious. But we embrace both. We faithfully and sincerely confess both. The former, that we may believe well; the latter, that we may live well. For he lives ill who does not believe well concerning God."[2]

These last words of his form a fitting transition to what we wish to say concerning certain other important teaching of S. Augustine, not directly connected with either of the three great controversies in which he was engaged. It would be leaving an essential part of our subject untouched, did we not at least draw attention to these other points of his teaching. And however obscure, or severe, or intensely dogmatic (in the popular abuse of that word) we may have found a part of what he says against the Pelagians, there is this to be taken into account, that *those doctrines are not all that is to be found in S. Augustine.* Indeed, many good judges and

[1] *De Civ. Dei*, v. 9. [2] *Id.* v. 10.

eminent theologians of the Church consider that in such a book as Canon Mozley's *Augustinian Doctrine of Predestination* there is a grave exaggeration of the place which predestination held in Augustine's great rich mind, as compared with other doctrines, — e.g. with that of sacramental grace. Certainly in him predestination and its allied truths are not everything, much as they have been made so by those who took the opportunity which, we own, he gave them, and built up harder walls and higher barriers than he ever did, to shut in their select systems. Let S. Augustine be devoutly read and studied and meditated upon, and his comprehensiveness will be perceived; and in his comprehensiveness is one element of his greatness.

To "*believe well concerning God,*" as he says in those words just quoted, expresses what was to him the foundation of religion. And his teaching concerning God is full of grand conception of what He is in His revelation of Himself to us, and of earnest counsel to us in our relations to Him. Many, in the freedom of thinking which is so rife to-day, refuse to accept any proper notion of God's sovereignty, and shrink with horror from what they conceive to be S. Augustine's idea of God as derived from the Anti-Pelagian writings. But even in those writings we maintain that his idea of God is *not* — as the author of *The Continuity of Christian Thought* says — that of "*absolute and arbitrary will* in which consists the only ground of right;"[1] as if He were "a bloodthirsty tyrant," "a horrible kind

[1] p. 171.

of divine Nero," as another writer puts it, who complacently declares, that S. Augustine "either did not see, or probably failed to appreciate the truth, that power, unbounded by considerations of justice, mercy, and goodness, is certainly arbitrary, and may be maleficent in its operations."[1] Neither of these, surely, are definitions of God which are justified by the writings against the Pelagians; and though the ideas of Almighty Power and Will are there made prominent, we can see how this naturally came to be from the conditions of the controversy, and he tells us the same in his own words. Moreover, if any are so troubled by his teaching on this point as to be driven to pervert it, what would they do with certain well known language of S. Paul's Epistles? Would they represent that this was *all his* teaching about God? Or would they throw out these so severe words, and re-construct the Bible? It might, perhaps, be thus better adapted to the Church which is no more than "the consentient reason of those who are enlightened by a divine teacher speaking within the soul!"[2]

S. Augustine, at all events, has other and fuller representations of God.[3] Let us briefly point out his teaching. The *Confessiones* is the work which will naturally be first suggested to most minds, as full of

[1] Owen's *Evenings with the Skeptics*, Vol. II. p. 195. [2] *Continuity* etc. p. 150. Cf. p. 30 of this *Essay*.

[3] Even Mr. Owen, with all his bitterness against dogma and the Church, as shown in his Essay on *The Skepticism of S. Augustine*, admits the exceptional value of Augustine's teaching about God, and admires its combined sublimity and versatility. Vid. *Evenings with the Skeptics*, Vol. II. pp. 191, 194, 515.

devout sentiment concerning God; yet its statements are equalled, if not excelled, by those of the *De Civitate Dei*, and the *De Trinitate*. He feels that he cannot speak of God, or worthily utter His praise, — for God is "unspeakable;" and even to call Him *so*, is "an opposition of words which is rather to be avoided by silence than explained away by speech."[1] "The clearer the sight of Him," even, "the less is the power of expression."[2] Yet, it is a step towards knowing what He is, to know what He is not.[3] God is incomprehensible;[4] yet we may know Him, — and the knowledge of Him is the sublimity of attainment.[5] He is in constant activity, in infinite space and time;[6] — there is *no growth* in His knowledge; His knowledge of past, present, future, is all one.[7] God is incomprehensible, yet to be ever sought,[8] — although the imperfection of *our knowing Him* be so great, compared with the perfection of *His knowing us*.[9] God is the Eternal Light, the *Truth*, the One alone *absolutely good;*[10] the "good of all good."[11] All others are to be loved *in God* and *for God*.[12] God alone satisfies;[13] He is Himself the great Reward, "the perfection of happiness, the sum of the happy life eternal."[14] "What then?" he asks, "hath

[1] *De Doc. Christ.* i. 6. Canon Freemantle calls this "S. Augustine's confession of Agnosticism"! *Bamp. Lect.* p. 436.
[2] *Con. Epis. Manich.* 21. [3] *De Trin.* viii. 3. [4] *De Trin.* xv. 2. [5] *De. Civ. Dei*, xi. 2. [6] *Id.* xi. 5. [7] *De Civ. Dei*, xi. 21; *De Trin.* xv. 13, 22. [8] *De Trin.* xv. 2, 49. [9] *Id.* ix. 1. [10] *De perfec. justit.* 32; *De nupt.* etc. ii. 48. [11] *De Trin.* viii. 4. [12] *Con. Faust.* xxii. 78; *Conf.* iv. 18. [13] *De Civ. Dei*, x. 25; *De Doc. Christ.* i. 35, 37. [14] *De Sp. et lit.* 37, 39; *De Civ. Dei*, xxii. 30.

God no reward? None, save Himself. The reward of God is God Himself."[1] And, as He is the chief good, it is our chief good to be united to Him.[2] We seek Him in vain through nature alone:— "Why do we go forth and run to the heights of the heavens and the lowest parts of the earth, seeking Him who is *within us*, if we wish to be with Him?"[3] — a remarkable utterance; for with all S. Augustine's teaching of the ethical transcendence of God, he taught His true *immanence;* and his writings are as much aglow with the thought of the nearness of God,[4] as they are with that of intense longing for Him. God must first be believed; we must believe, before we understand;[5] and on this point he has a wise caution;—"we must take care, lest the mind, believing that which it does not see, feign to itself something which is not, and hope for and love that which is false;"[6]—and then He is to be known and loved. "Who loves what he does not know? ... And what is it to know God, but to behold Him and steadfastly perceive Him with the mind?"[7] There is a striking passage upon the love of God and one's brother;— "Let no one say, I do not know what I love. Let him love his brother, and he will love the same love. For he knows the love with which he loves, more than the brother whom he loves. So now he can know God more than he knows his brother; clearly *known more, because more present; known more, because more within*

---

[1] *In Ps.* lxxii. 32. [2] *De Civ. Dei,* x. 3. [3] *De Trin.* viii. 11.
[4] *Conf.* iv. 18, 19; v. 2; vi. 4, 26; ix. 28. [5] *De Trin.* viii. 8. [6] *Id.* viii. 6. [7] *Id.*

him ; known more, because more certain. Embrace the love of God, and by love embrace God."[1] So believing, knowing, and loving Him, we must "rise to Him by spiritual conformity."[2] Tenderly and powerfully does Augustine urge our return to God, if we have strayed from Him ;— "In ourselves beholding His image, let us, like that younger son of the gospel, come to ourselves, and arise and return to Him from Whom by our sin we had departed. There our being will have no death, our knowledge no error, our love no mishap."[3]

Upon the great doctrine of the *Trinity*, S. Augustine is very full and strong, as we might expect from his having written so profound a treatise upon it ; in which, however, he rather traces types and resemblances in ourselves to the Triune nature, than assumes to give a purely argumentative proof, or to exhaust the full meaning of the doctrine.[4] In this work, as well as in the *De Doctrina Christiana*, he has language which has frequently been commented upon, as bearing striking resemblance to that of the Athanasian Creed.[5] The Holy Spirit, he teaches, proceeds from the Father and the Son :[6] He is "the unutterable communion" of Father and Son, yet *substance*, and of one substance with Father and Son.[7] He owns he cannot express the mystery, nor at all fathom the depths of God's nature.[8]

---

[1] *Id.* viii. 12.　[2] *De Civ. Dei*, ix. 18.　[3] *De Civ. Dei*, xi. 28.
[4] Vid. Haddan's *Preface* to the translation of the Edinburgh edition, p. vi.
[5] *De Trin.* v. 11 ; *De Doc. Christ.* i. 5.　[6] *De Trin.* iv. 29 ; xv. 29.
[7] *De Trin.* v. 12 ; vi. 7 ; vii. 6.　[8] *Id.* xv. 45.

Through the *Incarnation of our Lord*, he teaches, is our approach to God. The Son of God became Son of man, that sons of men might by grace become through Him sons of God.[1] Thus, we who have not the nature of God, and are yet partakers of God by His image which is in us, are brought nearer through the God-man.[2] This Incarnation is a true taking of humanity into the Divine Person of the Word:— "That nativity . . . conjoined, in the unity of the person, man to God, flesh to the Word."[3] "At the very moment that He began to be Man, He was nothing else than the Son of God ; . . . so Christ in one person unites the Word and man."[4] "So far as He is God, He and the Father are one; so far as He is man, the Father is greater than He."[5] This is "the Incarnation of the unchangeable Son of God, *whereby we are saved*."[6] It is the richest grace to us. "The grace of God could not have been more graciously commended to us, than thus, that the only Son of God, remaining unchangeable in Himself, should assume humanity;"[7]—and thus "He leads us straight to that Trinity by participation in which the angels themselves are blessed."[8] The Incarnation was to convince men of what seemed incredible.[9] It was to teach humility.[10] It was to demonstrate to man *his place in God's creation;*[11] to show "at how great a price God rated us, and how greatly He loved

---

[1] *De Civ. Dei*, xxi. 15. [2] *De Trin.* xiv. 11; cf. *De Civ. Dei*, xi. 2. [3] *De correp. et grat.* 30. [4] *Enchirid.* xxxvi. [5] *Id.* xxxv. [6] *De Civ. Dei*, x. 29. [7] *De Civ. Dei*, x. 29. [8] *Id.* ix. 15. [9] *De Trin.* xiii. 12. [10] *Id.* xiii. 22. [11] *Id.*

us."[1] Christ *the Mediator* is continually presented to our thought, mediating on earth and in heaven; "shedding His innocent blood for the remission of our sins,"[2] and that by a voluntary sacrifice;[3] — rising again, and taking His glorious Body up into the heavenly places.[4]

This Father has extensive teaching in relation to *The Angels*, — their creation, nature, relations to us present and future, etc., upon which we cannot dwell, but to which we will simply allude. A point of much interest is his belief that the angels who did not fall *shall never fall*, — have an eternal blessedness assured to them, as the reward of their fidelity;[5] and another, that the redeemed and saved among men are to make good the places, in bliss, of the angels who were lost.[6] Our earthliness prevents our nearer fellowship now with the holy angels;[7] to be ranked with them hereafter will be the height of our perfection.[8]

Of the teaching of S. Augustine upon *The Sacraments* and their grace we have already spoken to some extent, and have given many passages bearing upon the subject, especially in reference to Holy Baptism, as that subject came before us in treating of the Donatist controversy. But there is much more to be said; and the topic might worthily receive even much fuller con-

---

[1] *Id.* xiii. 13.   [2] *Id.* xiii. 18.   [3] *Id.* iv. 16.   [4] *De Civ. Dei*, x. 29.
[5] *Id.* xi. 13; xxii. 1.   [6] *Enchirid.* lxi.   [7] *De Civ. Dei*, viii. 25.

[8] *Con. Faust.* xxii. 28. In this connection it may be observed that S. Augustine has been severely criticised by some for departing from the earlier tradition in teaching that The Angel of the Lord in the Old Testament was not the Son of God. Vid. Medd's *One Mediator;* cf. Liddon's *Divinity of our Lord,* p. 55.

sideration than we now give it. Augustine often uses the word *sacrament* in its extended sense, as is common among the Fathers; — sometimes in a very loose way, e.g. distinguishing "the sacrament of baptism" from "the sacrament of conferring baptism."[1] He tersely contrasts the sacraments of the new with those of the old dispensation; the former, few, simple, majestic, sacred, "such, e.g. as the sacrament of baptism, and the celebration of the Body and Blood of the Lord."[2] Even as a visible symbol, for a bond of union, "their importance cannot be overstated, and only scoffers will treat them lightly."[3] In one passage he dwells upon the resemblance of sacraments to the things of which they are the sacraments, and says "if they had not such resemblance, they would not be sacraments at all;"[4] and continues, — "in most cases, moreover, they do, in virtue of this likeness, bear the names of the realities which they resemble:" — so, he says, "in a certain manner, the sacrament of Christ's Body is Christ's Body, and the sacrament of Christ's Blood is Christ's Blood;"[4] where the connection shows that he means to refer to the deep spiritual *mystery* of this sacrament. It is not a literal, carnal death, i.e. which takes place in the Eucharist; the death is sacramentally celebrated. "Was not Christ," he says, "once for all offered up in His own Person as a sacrifice? and yet, is He not likewise offered up in the sacrament as a sacrifice?"[4] In another place he well distinguishes

---

[1] *De Baptismo*, i. 2. [2] *De Doc. Christ.* iii. 13; *Con. Faust.* xix. 13, 14.
[3] *Con. Faust.* xix. 11. [4] *Ep.* xcviii. 9, *ad Bonifacium*.

between the outward and the inward; — "The material symbols are nothing else than visible speech, which, though sacred, is changeable and transitory. While God is eternal, the water of baptism and all that is material in the sacrament is transitory; the very word 'God,' which must be pronounced in the consecration, is a sound which passes in a moment. The actions and sounds pass away, but *their efficacy remains the same, and the spiritual gift thus communicated is eternal.*"[1] — In reference to the special grace of Baptism we venture to give one more passage in addition to those previously cited: — "This is the meaning of the great sacrament of baptism which is solemnized among us, that all who attain to this grace should *die to sin,* . . . and *rising from the font regenerate,* . . . should begin a new life in the Spirit, *whatever may be the age of the body,*"[2] — words which are strikingly like those of our Baptismal Offices. —— Referring now a little more fully to S. Augustine's Eucharistic teaching, — it may be observed that in his explanation of S. John vi. 53 ("except ye eat the flesh" etc.) in the *De Doctrina Christiana,* he at first appears to teach only the low and merely memorial significance of the Sacrament. He is illustrating the interpretation of figures and figurative expressions in Scripture. These words, he says, are "a figure, — enjoining that we should have a share in the sufferings of our Lord, and that we should retain a sweet and profitable memory of the fact that His flesh was wounded and crucified for us."[3] This is all true enough. But

[1] *Con. Faust.* xix. 16. [2] *Enchirid.* xlii. [3] *De Doctr. Christ.* iii. 24.

we must examine what further teaching he may have upon the Eucharist. He says in the *De Trinitate* (iii. 10) that "the fruits of the earth, consecrated by mystic prayer, and *received duly to our spiritual health*, are *sanctified* to become so great a sacrament *only by the Spirit of God* working invisibly." Here is the additional idea of the Divine power *accomplishing the consecration*, and making the Sacrament *Divine food* to us. There is *grace* in the Sacrament. In a passage of the *De Civitate Dei* (xvii. 20) there is a still fuller meaning. He is explaining the words — "Wisdom hath builded her an house" etc. "The Wisdom of God, the Word coeternal with the Father, hath builded Him an House, even a human body in the virgin womb, and hath subjoined the Church to it as members to an head, . . . hath furnished a table with wine and bread," etc. . . . "To be made partakers of this table is itself to begin to have life." . . . "This table . . . the Mediator of the New Testament Himself . . . *furnishes with His own Body and Blood.*" . . . "That sacrifice has succeeded all the sacrifices of the Old Testament." . . . "Instead of all these sacrifices and oblations *His Body is offered, and is served up to the partakers of it.*" Here is the distinct statement, that what we receive in the Sacrament, which was before taught to be spiritual food, is *the Body and Blood of the Lord*. Again, in the *De Civitate Dei* (xxi. 25) "What it is *in reality*, and not *sacramentally*, to eat His Body and drink His Blood," he says Christ Himself shows ; — "this is *to dwell in Christ*, that He also may dwell in us. It is as if He said, — he that dwelleth not in Me and in whom I do not dwell, let him not say or think that he eateth My Body or drinketh My Blood;"—words which justify the reference to Augustine in our Art. XXIX., as teaching that the wicked are in no wise partakers of *Christ*, although they sacramentally receive His Body. The passages cited are sufficient to show that the Real Presence of Christ in His Sacrament was the belief of S. Augustine. And as for such expressions, written elsewhere, as "Why make ready the teeth and the belly? Believe and thou hast eaten;" — "To believe on Him, this is to eat the living Bread," — they are in entire harmony with his other teaching; and moreover, if pressed, might go to establish the *reductio ad absurdum* that the Real Presence was not believed by even Paschasius himself, who once wrote "Christum vorari fas dentibus non est," — as of course every believer in the Real Presence would acknowledge.[1] — The *sacrifice* in the Eucharist he as plainly affirms; and presents as clearly as possible the great sacramental truth of the Church's offering of herself in and with the offering of the great High Priest. His definition of a true sacrifice is most excellent, as being "every work done that we may be united to God in holy fellowship, and which has reference to that supreme good and end in which alone we can be truly blessed;"[2] and his teaching is, that "the whole redeemed city, i.e. the congregation or community of the saints, *is offered to God as our sacrifice through the great High Priest*,

---

[1] Vid. *Ch. Quart. Rev.* Vol. IX. p. 209.   [2] *De Civ. Dei*, x. 6.

Who, that we might be members of this glorious Head, offered Himself to God in His Passion for us, in the form of a servant. . . . This is the sacrifice of Christians; we, being many, are one Body in Christ. And this also is the sacrifice *which the Church continually celebrates in the sacrament of the altar*, known to the faithful, in which she teaches that *she herself is offered in the offering she makes to God.*"[1]

Prayer for the faithful departed had been the custom of the Church long before S. Augustine's day. It is not strange, then, that we find direct and indirect teaching on this point in his works. When his holy mother, Monica, was taken from him, her dying request was this, "Lay my body anywhere, let not the care for it trouble you at all. This only I ask, that you will remember me at the Lord's altar wherever you be."[2] And he begs all who read his *Confessions* to thus remember her, — that so her last entreaty may be more abundantly fulfilled to her through the prayers of the many.[3] We find him also elsewhere teaching the benefit to the departed of prayers, and alms, and the Sacrament of the altar.[4] He affirms, however, as if guarding against the danger of a departure from primitive usage, that no prayer is of avail for those who die impenitent ; — "no one need hope that after he is dead he shall obtain merit with God which he has neglected to secure here ;"[5] — though he does condone the making of offerings for such, as a kind of comfort to the living.[6]

---

[1] *Id.* [2] *Confess.* ix. 27. [3] *Id.* ix. 37. [4] *Enchirid.* cx.; *De Civ. Dei*, xxi. 24, 27. [5] *Enchirid.* cx. [6] *Id.;* also vid. *Serm.* xxxii.

Not only prayer and sacrament for the departed are taught, but the prayers of the saints for us are invoked. "May he help us by his prayers," — he writes of S. Cyprian departed; and for this aid he says he longs.[1]

The Intermediate State, he teaches, is one in which "the soul dwells in a hidden retreat, where it enjoys rest or suffers affliction just in proportion to the merit it has earned by the life which it led on earth."[2] Connected with his teaching on this point is what he says upon the need of *cleansing* to the soul in this Intermediate State, and how far it is of avail. He writes in one place that souls "when purged from all contagion of corruption are placed in peaceful abodes until they take their bodies again."[3] Again he connects this cleansing with the Judgment; — "it appears . . . that some shall in the last Judgment suffer some kind of purgatorial punishments;"[4] though in another place his teaching is that we are not to "fancy that there are any purgatorial pains *except before* that final and dreadful judgment."[5] Some "shall not even suffer purgatorial torments after death."[6] He has a great deal to say in his writings, of the need of the soul's being cleansed, — purified, — that it may have power to see God: in this life "men see Him just so far as they die to this world; and so far as they live to it they see Him not;"[7] and he but carries his idea on to the other

---

[1] *De Baptismo*, v. 23; vii. 1. [2] *Enchirid.* cix. Stronger language is used in *De praedest. sanct.* 24. [3] *De Trin.* xv. 44. [4] *De Civ. Dei*, xx. 25. [5] *De Civ. Dei*, xxi. 13, 16. [6] *Id.* xxi. 16. [7] *De Doc. Christ.* i. 10; ii. 11.

world, in all that he says about purgatorial discipline; yet his doctrine is on the whole obscure. He more than once gives lengthy explanation of the text — "saved, yet so as by fire." He interprets the fire — of affliction, and grief, and tribulation; and then, after referring to a fire between death and the judgment, adds — "if it be said that [such] worldliness, being venial, shall be consumed in the fire of tribulation, either here only, or here and hereafter both, or here that it may not be hereafter, — *this I do not contradict, because possibly it is true.*"[1] He is not sure here; and in another work he shows the same uncertainty, and says "it is a matter that may be inquired into, and either ascertained or left doubtful, whether some believers shall pass through a kind of purgatorial fire after this life."[2]

Future punishment he believes to be eternal; and severely rebukes Origen (whom he says "the Church has condemned for this and other errors") for his wild fancy of restoring even the devil and his angels to the abodes of the blessed!"[3] He teaches "different degrees of punishment among the lost, as of glory among the saved." He inclines to the opinion that the fire of punishment is "material;"[4] but this is *only opinion*, while the doctrine itself he holds to be of *the faith;* and he solemnly declares, that "to be lost out of the kingdom of God, — to be an exile from the city of God, — *to be alienated from the life of God,*" — would be

---

[1] *De Civ. Dei*, xxi. 26.   [2] *Enchirid.* lxix.   [3] *De Civ. Dei*, xxi. 17.
[4] *De Civ. Dei*, xxi. 2.

incomparably greater punishment than any torments one can conceive of.[1]

The resurrection he believes is to be of the body of flesh, yet far different from the present mortal flesh;[2] a *spiritual* body,[3] of exceeding beauty and dignity;[4] — yet having the very same material as now, only differently arranged.[5]

The eternal felicity in the future life of the blessed he most eloquently describes; — that life "where necessity shall have no place, but full, certain, secure, everlasting felicity," where "there shall be the enjoyment of a beauty which appeals to reason," where "the body shall be forthwith wherever the spirit wills, and the spirit shall will nothing which is unbecoming either to the spirit or to the body," where "true honor" and true peace shall be, where there shall be "a higher freedom than that of the first man, who had the ability not to sin," even the highest freedom of will "*not able to sin;*" where "we shall rest and see, see and love, love and praise;" where "God Himself, Who is the Author of virtue, shall be its reward; for as there is nothing greater or better He has promised Himself;" where "we shall have eternal leisure to see that *He is God;* for we shall be full of Him, when He shall be all in all."[6]

In reference to all these many and varied teachings of the great Latin Father, we have thought it more just to let him speak for himself; and, though briefly

[1] *Enchirid.* cxii. [2] *De Civ. Dei*, xxi. 3, 8. [3] *Id.* xxii. 21.
[4] *Id.* xxii. 19, 24. [5] *Enchirid.* lxxxix. [6] *De Civ. Dei*, xxii. 30.

stating our opinion of his doctrine from point to point, to call careful attention rather to *what he actually taught.* And we would hope that our exposition has been fair to him, whose teaching we would have all Christian people, and especially all the clergy, reverently study. To thus study must be more and more to admire, and, within the bounds of Catholic truth, to gratefully accept. For, in spite of those hard theories and rigid reasonings of his about certain relations of God to man; as Maurice says, "the root of the matter was in him, an essential acknowledgment of God's absolute good-will, and *nearness to us*,"[1] and he wrought out these great principles with wondrous intellectual power, emotional fervor, and spiritual devotion.

What has been the influence of S. Augustine? How extensive has it been, — and has it been for good or ill? What is it likely to be? These are questions which will be variously answered, according to the standpoint of knowledge or sympathy. While he lived, that holy humble life, wherein worked a strong will, must have been a mighty factor of influence. The charge of hierarchical pretensions, which a few modern writers have unkindly brought against him, has no good warrant. Nor did his dogmatic earnestness in upholding doctrine, as Milman justly allows, indicate so much

[1] *Life* etc. Vol. II. p. 167. The reader may note how widely different is this estimate from that of the author of *The Continuity of Christian Thought.*

any "ambition of dictating to Christianity on these
abstruse topics," as "the desire of peace to his own
anxious spirit."[1] And the will has been well affirmed
to be no weak one, which wrought out his doctrines
into *a system*, and *an historical force*. His writings
went far and wide throughout Western and even into
Eastern Christendom; and, as they spread, his opinions gained an increasing influence. At the close of
his career of nearly forty years as priest and Bishop in
Hippo, he had successfully met the errors of Manichaeism and Donatism, and had broken the delusive spell
of Pelagianism; and in his writings as a whole had so
established the claims of the Christian Church, and so
formulated Christian doctrine, as to have achieved the
position of *leader of the thought of the Christian world*.
Easily and admittedly the superior of all the Fathers of
the West, in any age, — Ambrose, Jerome, Gregory; —
he need not be compared with his great predecessors
in the East, while he was then manifestly far above all
his contemporaries.[2]

Yet even that greatness was not a perfect ideal.
The discussions which had sprung up all about him
during the few last years of his life, the replies which
he had been obliged to make upon this or that point of
doctrine, to satisfy the questionings of those who desired
to go all lengths with him in his beliefs, or to meet the
bolder and bolder attacks of some open enemy, show

---

[1] *History of Christianity*, Vol. III. p. 177.

[2] S. Athanasius can hardly be called a contemporary of S. Augustine. He died in the year 373, when S. Augustine was not yet twenty years old.

the vitality which still thrived in the error which he had been so long opposing, and are also a pointed comment upon the imperfection of any human system. Pelagianism or Semi-Pelagianism was not yet dead: it had truth with its error. Augustine must reason, and restrict, and define; he must save his human theories; he must carry his philosophical speculations up into the mysteries of God's Being. The inquiries and the opposition had come chiefly from Southern Gaul and from certain parts of Italy; and soon after his death they took more and more definite shape of hostility against *Predestinarianism*,[1] as fatalistic, derogatory to the mercy of God, and destroying the responsibility of man. To this period belongs the supposed protest of Vincent of Lerins, the "*semper, ubique, et ab omnibus*," very likely meant to meet Augustine on his own ground.[2] The controversy which had thus sprung up anew, and was bitterly carried on for a century, was at length settled largely through the influence of Caesarius, Archbishop of Arles, by a local council which he held for his province, in Orange, in A.D. 529. This council (of fourteen Bishops) formally adopted a series of articles which Caesarius had received from Rome. These articles are strong in their condemnation of Pelagianism and Semi-Pelagianism,

[1] Especially any *predestination to evil*, which some deduced from S. Augustine's doctrine.

[2] Vid. Neander, *Ch. Hist.* Vol. II. p. 696; and compare the passage in the *De Util. Cred.* 31, — "This therefore I have believed, trusting to report strengthened by numbers (*ab omnibus*), agreement (*ubique*), antiquity" (*semper*).

and draw most of their authority directly from the works of S. Augustine ; but they do not mention predestination to life, — and thus they show a "cautious and discriminating adhesion;"[1] while they go on to declare the capability of all the baptized, by Christ's aid and coöperation, to fulfil the conditions of salvation, and they anathematize *all who hold that any are "predestinated to evil by divine power."*[2] Thus, as says Canon Bright, "this little Gallican Council earned the respect and gratitude of ages, for having brought a great question to a comprehensive settlement, and preserved the Christianity of Western Europe from a one-sidedness baneful to its soul-attracting power."[3]

We are brought, then, to the fact of *a serious modification of Augustine's doctrine*, as accepted by the Latins ; — a modification which has ever since shaped the authoritative attitude of the Roman Church towards his teaching. Modified or unmodified, that doctrine reigned supreme throughout the West for a thousand years, down to the time of the Continental Reformation. And it may be owned, that, under the darkness and ignorance and superstition of the Middle Ages, it was not, as a system, an unmixed good. With a sense of sin overpowering and deepening, — something which he had taught them, — men kept dwelling too much upon *one part* of the Augustinian teaching about God

[1] Canon Bright's *Introduction* etc. ut sup. p. lxv.
[2] The Acts of the Second Council of Orange are given at the close of Canon Bright's valuable edition of *The Anti-Pelagian Treatises*, pp. 384–392.
[3] *Introduction* etc. p. lxvi.

and His government of the world. All classes of people, too, in blind submission to authority, were coming too much under the sway of that one master-mind. "Augustinum, quem contradicere *fas non est*," says Paschasius:—his authority was put next to the Bible,[1] perhaps equal or superior to it, by many: it was too much influence for any one system; it was making man master of conscience and of life.

Gregory the Great was the first distinguished disciple of S. Augustine; and his writings breathe the devout spirit of his master, and take almost his very thought and language.[2] Sometimes, in doctrine, he goes beyond him; noticeably, in the direction of mediaeval Romanism, in reference to purgatory.[3] But it was in *Scholasticism* that the influence of S. Augustine was more extensively known. Among the schoolmen, S. Bernard, S. Anselm, and S. Thomas Aquinas are those who chiefly maintained and developed his teaching;—preeminent among them all is S. Thomas. He is universally acknowledged as the great theologian of the middle ages; and his complex system, so rich in thought, with its doctrines of free-will, and necessity, and divine power, and predestination, and creation, and grace, is directly built up upon the Augustinian foundation,—with added original features, and modifications to some extent of Augustine's accredited severity, especially in

[1] Vid. Poole's *Illustrations of the History of Mediaeval Thought*, p. 174.

[2] Cf. *Moral.* xx. 1; and vid. what Abp. Trench says of "the influence of Gregory's great teacher." *S. Augustine as an Interpreter* etc. ut sup. p. 13.

[3] Vid. Hardwick's *Middle Age*, pp. 62-64, and notes.

reference to predestination.¹ All this might be developed with great interest in a fuller consideration of the subject than we have aimed to give in this monograph.

At the time of the Reformation in the sixteenth century, the Roman Church is supposed to have lost much of its active interest, to say the least, in the doctrines of the great Latin Father, owing to the way in which they were used or abused by the Reformers. The decrees of the Council of Trent, in part, show this. The *shaping* of those decrees was largely the work of the Jesuits, whose theology was a direct reaction from Luther's opinions, which were presumed to be based upon the teachings of S. Augustine. But, on the other hand, it is to be said that Luther may have *misunderstood or perverted S. Augustine*, as assuredly Jansenius, in the next century, *exaggerated and perverted S. Augustine:* and that certainly the Roman Church so considered it, and in its condemnation of Jansenism *did not thereby necessarily condemn Augustinian doctrine.* In fact, the Roman Church to-day would not venture to exclude that doctrine "from the pale of tolerated opinion;"² much as she might like to do so because of some of his teachings, which directly militate against her own claims.

Although the unquestioned dominion of S. Augustine was broken in the convulsions of the sixteenth century,

---

¹ For these modifications, vid. Mozley's *Augustinian Doctrine* etc. p. 285, et seq.

² Canon Mozley, we think, could scarcely make good his words on p. 226, n. of the *Augustinian Doctrine* etc.

it is commonly said that his influence has lived since then in the opinions of the great Reformers, — in those of Luther, and still more in those of Calvin. And this is true ; and yet, we should claim, not precisely in the way in which the descendants and disciples of those men would say. S. Augustine did influence, and influence profoundly, both Luther and Calvin ; and we thank God for all the *good influence* which his Catholic doctrine had upon them ; but, unfortunately, it was, far more, certain of his exaggerations of doctrine which influenced them, which they then exaggerated to a still greater degree ; so that the question becomes, *How far is Lutheranism or Calvinism a fair reproduction of the teachings of S. Augustine ?*

A full answer to this question cannot be given within our present limits : but a few points may be noted. Luther made S. Augustine his great teacher in theology.[1] And in his writings he has not only reproduced much of the thought of his teacher, but has handed down to modern times — that which but for him they might not have so fully known — a breathing forth, if I may call it, of the Augustinian spirit. Yet all along we have to distinguish that spirit from the spirit of his own teachings, — and often in most important doctrines. His doctrine of *original sin*, e.g. was very different from that of Augustine. He taught that man was so utterly ruined by the Fall, that the operation of God's Spirit in him finds as little response as in a brute

[1] To William of Occam he owed his theory of *Consubstantiation* in the Eucharist.

or a devil. Here are some of his words: — "The intellectual faculties are not only corrupted, but they are *totally annihilated by sin in man exactly the same as in devils;* so that in them there is nothing but a corrupt spirit, a perverse will, hostile to God in everything."[1] This is not, if we apprehend it, the Augustinian doctrine, which makes so much of the Image of God still remaining in man. Again, such a view of original sin would bid Luther, as he did, deny all *freedom of the will.* As he teaches, — "In spiritual and divine things, man is as the pillar of salt into which Lot's wife was turned; yea, he is like a stick or a stone, which is lifeless, etc."[2] "Free-will, after original sin, is a mere name,"[3] he says. But S. Augustine, as we think we have fully shown, whatever may be made of his theoretical distinctions, did not at all deny the practical freedom of the will, and the responsibility which flowed therefrom. Luther made *justification* only a judicial act of God, delivering from the punishment of sin, but not from sin itself. All righteousness is external to us;[4] is such a literal imputation of Christ's righteousness, as to make His righteousness and obedience ours; which subverts Christian morality. S. Augustine, teaching that they are "justified in Christ who believe in Him, by a secret communion and inspiration of spiritual grace, which makes every one who cleaves to the Lord 'one spirit' with Him,"[5] does not go

[1] Ed. Wittenberg, i. 99. [2] *In Genes.* chap. xix. [3] In the *Paradoxes;* Vid. Hardwick's *Reformation*, p. 29. [4] *Solid. Declar.* iii. *de Fid. Justif.* § 11, § 48. [5] *De peccat. merit.* i. 11.

anything like as far as Luther; and appears to present a very different doctrine. With him, it is rather the Power of Christ dwelling in us, His Life working in us, whereby we cleave to Him, and produce good works.[1] But the main distinction appears in reference to Luther's all-controlling tenet of *Justification by faith*. This was held in such a way as almost to exclude repentance, to exclude good works, to make faith amount to *assurance*. Justification by faith only, he was never tired of proclaiming. "He is not justified who does many works, but he who without any work has much faith in Christ."[2] And what does his theory of faith become? A man has faith "*when he believes that he has been received by God into grace;*"[3] faith, then, is *assurance;* when I believe I am saved, I am saved, by this "self-confident assurance of individual interest in Christ's sacrifice," which Mr. Sadler well describes as "foreclosing a man's probation the moment he believes, or thinks he believes"![4] And the dreadful carrying out of this doctrine of *faith only* into its relation to sin cannot be disguised nor explained away:—"Be a sinner," says Luther, "and sin stoutly" ("*esto peccator; et pecca fortiter,*")—"but the more bravely trust and rejoice in Christ, Who is the conqueror of sin, death, and the world. Here *we must sin*, as long as we live," ("*peccandum est, quamdiu sic*

---

[1] For some most valuable teaching upon this aspect of justification, vid. Sadler's *Justification of Life*, pp. 339, 347, etc.

[2] *Paradoxes*.   [3] *Augsburg Confession*, Art. iv.   [4] *Justification of Life*, pp. 74, 209.

sumus.") . . . From Him sin shall not separate us, though we commit whoredom or murder a thousand thousand times in one day. Thinkest thou that the price and redemption offered for our sins by this Divine Lamb is so small that it cannot avail to cover your *sham sins?* Pray boldly; thou art a most bold sinner." ("*Ora fortiter; es enim fortissimus peccator.*")[1] Need we say that S. Augustine has nothing like all this? Faith *alone*, with him, means alone as against nature or the law; as where he says that "nothing but belief in the Mediator saved the saints of the Old Testament;"[2] or as against works done in our own strength alone; as in that decisive passage where he commends the one of few works and great faith, and declares that "he shall be delivered for this life, and depart to be received into the company of those who shall reign with Christ."[3] And can any passage be found, where he is so carried away by ideas of faith, or grace, as to utter the shocking sentiments of Luther? Faith in Christ, he tells us, will give us true righteousness,— and by this power we can gain victory over sin. By this "*love of God*" working in us vices are to be overcome. "We must declare war upon them, and wage this war keenly, *lest we be landed in damnable sins.*" Thus only can we come to "the end of this war," and "the well-ordered peace" for which we long.[4]

---

[1] Given in the late Dr. Mill's *Five Sermons on the Nature of Christianity;* notes, p. 131-2.

[2] *Con. duas literas* etc. i. 39.   [3] *Con. duas literas* etc. iii. 14.   [4] *De Civ. Dei*, xxi. 15, 16.

As regards Calvin, very different observations need to be made, although in some ways he and Luther were alike in their reproduction and perversion of S. Augustine. Calvin had a more just view than Luther of *original sin*, and admitted some degree of human coöperation.[1] Calvin's view of *assurance* was like Luther's. "Joined to Christ, the believer has life in Him, and *knows that he is saved.*" Calvin, however, with his strong logical mind, used the influence of S. Augustine, far more than Luther ever did or could, in forming a system. That system was built up upon *absolute predestination.* And here he went far beyond even the strictest Augustinian statements; and propounded a theory which not only has to do with both saved and lost, (and it is an open question how far Augustine taught *the predestination of the lost*) but also denies regenerating grace to the baptized. Baptism is only "obsignatory" of grace which one already had if he were a child of grace, one of the elect.[2] If not, he only partakes of the material element. This is radically different from S. Augustine's teaching, which is that all the worthily baptized are truly *regenerate*, and thus partakers of grace; though we cannot say who of them are predestinated, and will finally attain to perseverance. Moreover, Calvin affirms that " God intentionally produces within those who are not elect *an apparent faith;* that He insinuates Himself into the souls of the reprobate, in order to render them less excusable"![3] We have yet to find a parallel

[1] *Instit. lib.* ii. c. 3. [2] Hardwick's *Reformation*, pp. 130, 176.
[3] *Instit.* l. iii. c. 2, n. 11.

to anything like this in S. Augustine. With all his rigidity, tenderness is manifest. God permits evil, in justice;[1] but only that He may bring out of it greater good;[2] and those who commit the greatest evil are not estranged from His goodness.[3] He cannot explain God's decrees. They are inscrutable. But there he stops: he leaves them a mystery; bidding us not question nor complain; and again and again taking up the refrain, "*O altitudo!*"

Thus we have endeavored to suggest that while both Luther and Calvin deeply felt the influence of S. Augustine, and to a degree handed on that influence to those who came after them, they did not always appreciate or follow it; and so they must not by any means always be taken fairly to represent him. As Hardwick writes, in reference to the influence of the Calvinists in the Lambeth Articles, — they so "exaggerated, and curtailed, and contradicted," that even with much "similarity of language" they wrought "a profound if not a fundamental change" in the teaching of Augustine.[4] The modern world should never be suffered to forget that *what is Lutheran or Calvinistic is not necessarily Augustinian.* How far S. Augustine is responsible for their mistakes, is a question too deep and complex for man to answer. He gave them the opportunity, as we have already admitted. Moreover, the rejection of their errors is not always seen to have the purest motive. In the re-action of our day from

[1] *Enchirid.* xcvi.; *De Trin.* xiii. 16.   [2] *Enchirid.* xxvii.; *De Civ. Dei*, xxii. 1.   [3] *De Trin.* xiii. 16.   [4] *History of the Articles*, p. 164.

the "mischief" — so called — of Calvinism, we may observe, with trained vision, both a recoil from a narrowing and base bondage, which God never appointed; and also a desire for a freedom which is lawlessness and license. In the modern Reformers, and in the ancient Saint and Father, let us *take the Catholic truth, and throw away the individual error.*

A special study might be made of the influence of S. Augustine upon our own Prayer-Book and Articles. Much of the thought and even of the exact language of the Articles, as we have hinted, is his. The Articles, as we now possess them, have a history; and that history makes known many changes from severity to moderation and cautiousness of statement; and in effecting these changes, their teaching has become not so much that of Calvin as that of Luther, and not so much that of Luther as that of S. Augustine.[1] But we are more interested in the teaching of the Services. Directly or indirectly, — in their statements concerning God and man, sin and grace, faith and good works, the constitution and authority of the Church, and the blessing of the Sacraments, — *their teaching is Augustinian.* It is read in the Ordinal, in the

[1] For the teaching and much of the very language of Articles IX., X., XI., XII., XVII., XXV., XXVI., XXVII., XXIX., the reader may consult *De nupt. et concupis.* i. 28, ii 45; *De peccat. remiss.* ii. 44, 45; *De fid. et oper.* 14, *De Baptismo*, passim; *Tract.* xxvi. in S. John Ev. § 18; in addition to the many passages already given which have a clear bearing upon the composition of the Articles. Bp. Forbes, of Brechin, calls the Seventeenth Article "a concise summary of S. Augustine's teaching" upon predestination.

Liturgy, in the Baptismal Offices, in the Daily Offices, and in the Collects. Very naturally much of this teaching has felt the moulding of the Continental Reformation; but even that portion did not conform itself to sixteenth century models; while much was taken direct from ancient service-books, — as e.g. two-thirds of the Collects which come from the Sacramentaries of Gregory and Gelasius and Leo; and it is worthy of note how fully, in her reverting to primitive Catholicity, the Anglican Church was satisfied *to go back only to S. Augustine*. And this, we would believe, was not from a blind subjection to him; nor from failure to discover some purer or more Catholic doctrine, of more remote East, or nearer West; nor *only* was it because S. Augustine had been the first to formulate dogmatic teaching, and his influence had permeated others, as a Gregory, or a Leo; but because the Augustinian teaching was seen to mirror, so fully and faithfully, that of *the Word of God and primitive antiquity*.

Thus much concerning *the return to S. Augustine* may fit us to look forward a little, and say in few words, what we think is likely to be his influence in the future. His influence is fairly established in the present; — insecurely perhaps, in the outside world of sect and dissent, because of the many Lutheran and Calvinistic modifications; though even *there* with increasing stability, from the very law of God's truth refining itself away from error; but surely, firmly, grandly, in the historic Church of Christ. And everywhere this is so evident, that the author who so deprecates "the lingering hold of Augustine upon the modern mind" deems it so "formidable an obstacle" that it will need "an intellectual revolution"[1] to shake us from this subjection and bring us back to freedom. We have sufficiently shown why we think such a revolution is not likely soon to take place; why we deem the certainty of the present the best promise for the future. Nor can we consider the rejection of his teaching anything less than perilous to the best interests of Christianity in the world. God raised up this man for a great work in the world; and that work is not accomplished. It has abiding elements, which belong to humanity. S. Augustine is as much needed as ever; and he will continue to be needed, — both negatively, against Manichaeans, and Donatists, and Pelagians, and Semi-Pelagians; and positively, for the great teachings of grace in the One Name and the One Church. He is not in reality in contradiction with the more primitive East; nor is he alien to the best spirit of the modern world. He saves Christianity from the dreamy speculations of the East; while he teaches us all better to know ourselves, and our destiny in God. To Him he guides us; and to Him, our God, we would make his teaching lead us; — with his own words on our lips and in our hearts, for faith and obedience, for devotion and peace: — "*Da quod jubes, et jube quod vis.*" "*Fecisti nos ad Te; et inquietum est cor nostrum, donec requiescat in Te.*"

[1] *Continuity of Christian Thought*, p. 11.

www.ingramcontent.com/pod-product-compliance
Lightning Source LLC
Chambersburg PA
CBHW020153170426
43199CB00010B/1014